Pastels

From the 16th to the 20th century

Pastels

From the 16th to the 20th century

by

Geneviève Monnier

© 1984 by Editions d'Art Albert Skira S.A., Geneva

Reproduction rights reserved by S.P.A.D.E.M.,
Paris, and Cosmopress, Geneva

Published in the U.S.A. by
Rizzoli International Publications, New York
ISBN 0-8478-0533-6

Published in Great Britain by
Macmillan London Ltd.
ISBN 0-333-37066-X

Printed and bound in Switzerland

Library of Congress Cataloging in Publication Data

Monnier, Geneviève.
    Pastels: from the 16th to the 20th century.

    Translation of Le pastel.
    Bibliography: p.
    Includes index.
    1. Pastel drawing-History. I. Title.
NC880.M6613   1984   741.2 35 09   83-51582
ISBN 0-8478-0533-6

Contents

Introduction

Pastel: powdered colour with an infinite range of shades and gradations, of unfading freshness and intensity, spanning more than 1650 nuances of the colour spectrum, and peculiarly fitted for ease and rapidity of handling, immediate transcription of an emotion or idea, easily effaced, easily re-worked and blended. The pigments can be rubbed in, made luminous and velvety, or given a soft and silky matness of grain. Pastel is line and colour at once. It can also be built up into rich skeins of blended lines, into rapid jottings of all colours creating a dense and brilliant texture.

Some artists have used it for its hazy and vaporous qualities, its effects of stumping and rubbing (Nanteuil, Vivien, La Tour, Nattier, Liotard, Aman-Jean, Loup, Ernest Laurent), others for its vigorous outlines and hatchings (Chardin, Picasso). Many draughtsmen have combined and endlessly va-ried the ambivalence of these possibilities: Perronneau working over a modelled figure with the stump and setting it off with green shadings, Degas integrating colour streaks, vaporizations and gumming, Henri Michaux superimposing and interweaving imprints and rubbings. For pas-tel is a medium of unsuspected range and diversity. It is spirited, variegated, ever changing, the strokes running straight or zigzagging, breaking into dottings or commas or sweeping curves, hatched with fine parallels or broad squashings, interweaving from top to bottom or left to right, or ef-faced by rubbing and scraping.

Being so light and dry, pastel pigments present the problem of securing their adhesion to the ground. All the artists who have used the medium, from its beginnings, have had to face this practical difficulty and choose the fixative whose chemical ingredients seemed least likely to alter the texture and the image; even the best fixatives available today reduce the brilliance and modify the equilibrium of the colours.

Intent on drawing in black and white with pencil, Conté crayon or char-coal, some draughtsmen, like Seurat, have never used colour in their works on paper. Others used pastel on rare occasions, usually giving preference to the powdery grain of the charcoal stick, like Julio Gonzalez, Max Ernst, Hartung. Some, like Redon, have begun by working extensively in char-coal (these drawings he called his *Blacks*), before going on, with unflag-ging intentness, to pastel colours. Sometimes pastel only appears in an artist's work for a brief period, for a few years, or in a few sequences, or at the very end of his life-work, as with Chardin.

The works reproduced here have been chosen with a view to presenting pastel rather as a methodical exercise and a continuous line of research. It is curious to note a distinct cleavage between the artists who practise wash drawing, watercolour or gouache and those who prefer pastel with its dry pigments. Poussin, Claude Lorrain, Turner, Fuseli, Géricault, Cézanne and Kandinsky produced a large body of wash drawings or watercolours but did not use pastel, or used it only very occasionally. Similarly one cannot help noticing the large number of artists who like to work with coloured crayons or watercolour but ignore pastel (or take it up very rarely): Ensor, Kubin, Lindner, Moore, Alechinsky, Buri, Hockney, Dewasne, Sol LeWitt. Nevertheless, at every period there are a few men who seem to have made a point of trying out every medium available to the artist, including pastel: Leonardo da Vinci, Barocci, Boucher, Degas, Klimt, Rouault, Picasso, Kokoschka, Masson, Miró, Frank Stella.

From the beginning, approaching their themes with a naturalistic simplicity, pastel painters were concerned with the representation of narrative images and their details: the study of a face or a silhouette, the sketch of a portrait. Then the various elements were organized on the picture surface, creating a better ordered relation between figure and setting, and developing the scene as a whole. The transcription of reality, of objects and accessories, recording a moment or an instant, serves to identify the life of a society, including its anecdotes, spelled out in these fixed images, in these attitudes quickened by the play of light and composed in space. These works are not only portraits but also interiors and outdoor scenes, street scenes and landscapes. They show different approaches to a representation of the world, but all are meant to be accurate and truthful. They aim at conveying, by way of the portrait setting, a certain idea of man, of his function, profession and social standing.

For all the variety of their style, lifelikeness was the initial purpose of all these portraits, some of them more or less remote from reality, some worked up in ritual poses, some evoking home life. The elaborate costumes and pompous setting and attitudes confront us with the prototype of the official portrait, which appears in the early eighteenth century just as a larger picture format was coming into fashion. All the effigies of kings, princes and princesses were conceived on this same pattern by the artists of following generations: haughty poses, showy costumes, ermine mantles. The solemnity of this court art is common to all Europe in the seventeenth and eighteenth centuries. At first the personage often leans on his sword pommel or cane; later he is usually seen in half-length, seated and leaning on a table or over a book. The tendency was towards a freer pose, a more familiar, more intimist attitude.

Magistrates, burghers, artists, musicians and philosophers are recorded for posterity at a telling moment of their professional life, as suggested by an open book, a manuscript, a portfolio of drawings, a print, a letter, a pen-holder, a musical score.

The allegorical and mythological portrait, sometimes real, sometimes imaginary, but always pointedly decorative, was developed and refined in the eighteenth century in Italy and France, its fanciful figures and "capriccios" being combined with genre subjects deriving from Dutch painting. In the latter half of the eighteenth century (with Perronneau and Chardin) there comes a fresh emphasis on realism, naturalness, sincerity; affectation and abundance of accessories are less in evidence; the artist is more concerned with the texture and colours of pastel. This shift of taste brought with it something more of spontaneity, picturesqueness and intimism, before the return to a new minuteness of treatment, as seen in the rare Neo-classical portraits in pastel, whose cold perfection is better suited to oil painting, wash drawing or black chalk.

With the Romantic painters pastel again comes to the fore. The intensity of the colours and the dramatic emotion of faces and gestures command attention (Delacroix).

For the Impressionists, pastel offered a medium well suited to recording the sudden excitement of visual sensations, the fresh colours of nature and fleeting effects of light. The fragility of its texture corresponded to the evanescence of sense perceptions: Manet, Monet, Sisley, Pissarro, Renoir, Guillaumin, Caillebotte. Pastel was equally well suited to fixing a snapshot image. Degas focused his eye on new and marginal figures (jockeys, dancers, women in their bath, laundresses, milliners), approaching them closely and observing their every gesture from every side. With his odd angles of focus and off-centre composition, he marks a decisive break with long-standing traditions of pictorial representation.

While the portrait, in its earlier form, was like a factual statement, offering an overall view slightly distanced from the sitter, by the latter half of the nineteenth century, with Millet and Degas, it had undergone a radical change, being brought into focus in close-up with ever subtler effects of daylight or artificial light.

The other innovation made by Degas, and one that opened a whole new field for the twentieth century, was his use of mixed media. In his ceaseless efforts to build up his interblending, variously textured layers of colours, he would resort to one medium after another in the same work, combining pastel, gouache, tempera and oils diluted with turpentine. Whether used as a dry pigment or mixed with water, pastel permitted an endless reworking of the details of his compositions. It was Degas's momentous innovation that he did away with the old distinctions between powdered pigments and brushwork, between the craft of the draughtsman and that of the painter.

For the Symbolists pastel was no longer a means of recording reality, but rather a means of expressing the inner life, the world of dreams, of imagination, of the unconscious. The themes changed accordingly, and so did their titles: Silence, Meditation, Solitude, Melancholy. The portrait and the self-portrait remained important subjects, but they were treated rather as evocations or disquieting apparitions. The Symbolists cultivated an art of calculated haziness, of soft-focus effects, in order to give a sense of mystery to their scenes. With them a single colour often predominates, becoming indeed the essential subject of the picture. Their concern was the picture for its own sake, not the representation of something outside it, and they used the arabesque for decorative purposes. In this, and in their exploration of the expressive power of colour, emotion and distortion, they brought their influence to bear on early twentieth-century art, marking both the Fauves and the Expressionists (Kirchner).

One of the first to use colour as a vector leading directly to abstraction was Kupka, who juxtaposed colour patches (based on the laws of simultaneous contrasts) according to a rhythmic and linear pattern. Then, increasingly set free from any descriptive function, colour surged forward, following the explosion of the imagination (Miró, Klee). With Masson it reached a paroxysm of intensity resoundingly punctuated by the same gestural violence that we find in Pollock. For Gorky and de Kooning pastel was flexible enough to keep up with all the metamorphoses of form and handling. In the hands of the Surrealists pastel was a further vehicle of transgression, in the often bewildering shape of composite images, recreated spaces, iridescent colours. The alternation or coexistence between imagination, abstraction and narration has continued throughout the twentieth century. In the past thirty years or so another of the many formal possibilities of pastel has been worked out: the calligraphic abstraction of rhythmic patterns as various as those of Atlan, Hartung, Riopelle, Twombly. Other possibilities in course of being realized are the juxtaposition of colours or the unification of tones and their mixtures on a picture surface whose textural variety can be developed *ad infinitum* through colour patches, areas of flat colour, fluid arabesques and geometric patterning. Meanwhile, in the use of pastel, certain characteristics remain unchanged, like the intensity of its colour and the matt effect of its pigment grain, magical because multiform.

From the 16th to the 18th century

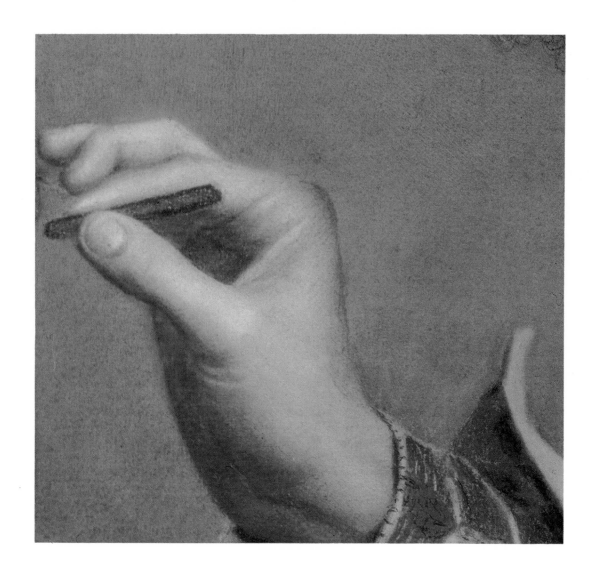

A new technique for drawing in brighter colours

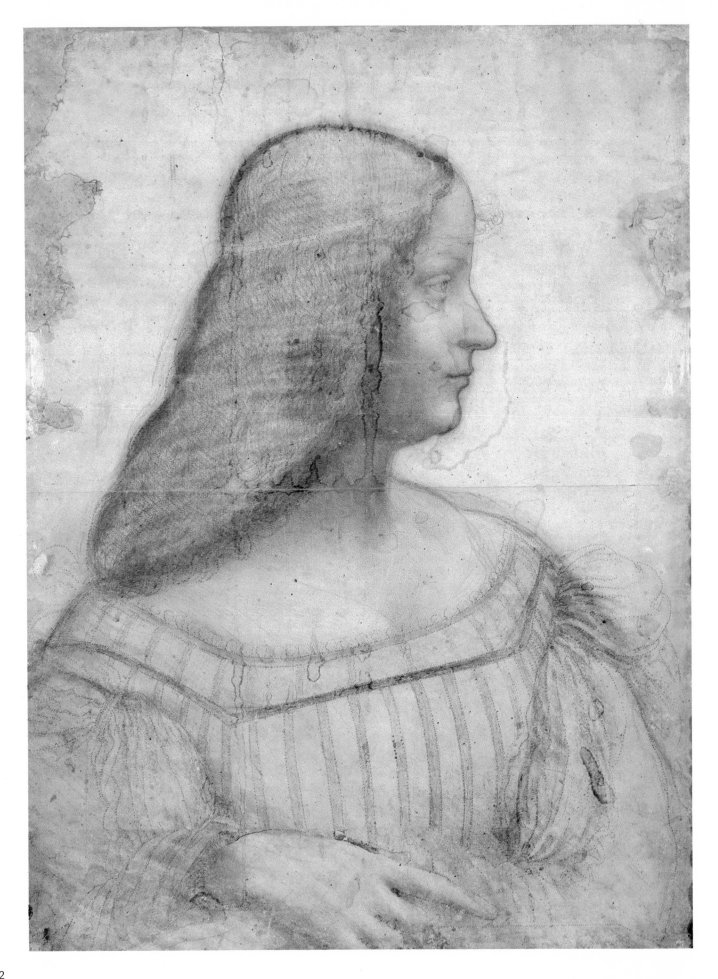

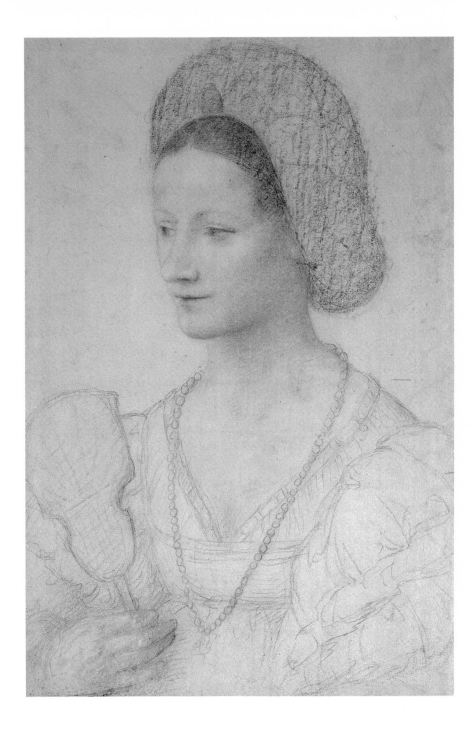

Leonardo da Vinci
(1452-1519)
Supposed Portrait of
Isabella d'Este, Duchess of Mantua, 1499.
Black and red chalk and pastel.

Bernardino Luini
(c. 1481-1532)
Portrait of a Lady.
Black chalk and coloured crayons
heightened with pastel.

The etymology of the word pastel (*pastello*, from *pasta*, paste) would suggest an Italian origin. But Leonardo da Vinci, in referring to this technique, which he calls the "dry colouring method" (folio 247, *Codice Atlantico*, Biblioteca Ambrosiana, Milan), says he learned it from a French artist, Jean Perréal, who came to Milan in 1499 with Louis XII. That same year, in December 1499, at Mantua, Leonardo is said to have executed his famous portrait drawing of *Isabella d'Este, Duchess of Mantua*, a preparatory study in black and red chalk heightened with golden yellow pastel on cardboard; the contours are pricked for transfer, but the final portrait was never painted.

Pastel was applied here only in light touches, to set off with yellow the neck line of the dress and shade with brown the mass of falling hair. This study is a rare example of its kind; very few

have come down from this period around the turn of the fifteenth and sixteenth centuries. It is the prototype of the portraits that were to be painted in the following century: bust slanting away in three-quarter view, head in profile, in close-up; sometimes, as in Bernardino Luini, one hand is visible in the foreground. The idea of pastel heightening was taken over and amplified by Leonardo's collaborators and pupils. The *Portrait of a Lady* is a drawing that was long attributed to Leonardo himself, until it was related to Bernardino Luini's painting of a *Young Woman* (National Gallery, Washington). Slight touches of colour, pink and white for the flesh tints of the face, yellow and brown for the hair, go to build up the figure in the drawing, supple and vibrant with life. Throughout the sixteenth century pastel was used to heighten portrait drawings with a light toning of colour.

There was a large output in France of these so-called three-crayon portraits, drawn in black and red chalk, highlights being added with white chalk; this combination made possible a wide range and variety of modulations. Black chalk is usually the predominant medium, red chalk being added to fill out and define, with a few apt touches, the eyes, nose, lips and ears; it was also used as a light rubbing, to suggest the flesh tints of the face.

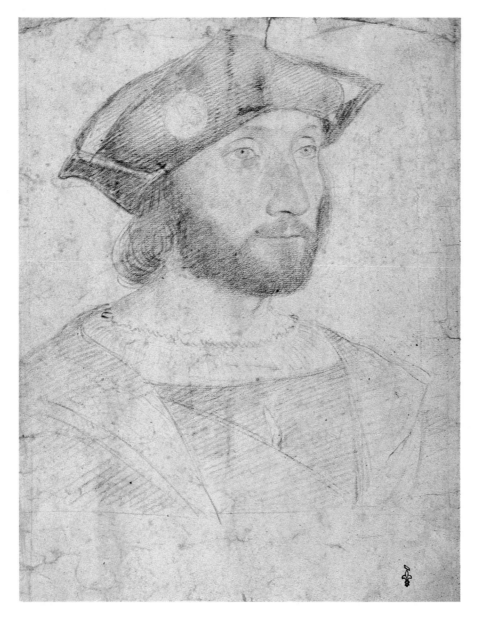

Jean Clouet
(c. 1485-1541)
Admiral Bonnivet.
Black and red chalk and pastel.

But the colouring of these three-crayon portraits is always very subdued. So that, beginning with the early examples shown here, one can understand the appeal exerted by pastel sticks, permitting as they did a wide range of tonal nuances. Pastel also lent itself to unusual textural effects, being more flexible, more vaporous; it more readily permitted shading and rubbing out, reworking and the superimposing of successive layers of colours.

The *Portrait of a Lady* attributed to Daniel Dumonstier is worked out in minute detail, searchingly explored and rendered with serried modelling: facial features are laid in with black chalk and then heightened with colours. The numbering in the upper right corner (a figure 6) indicates that this sheet must have been one of a set of portraits dating to about 1630-1633.

The *Portrait of a Young Woman Holding a Cat*, attributed to

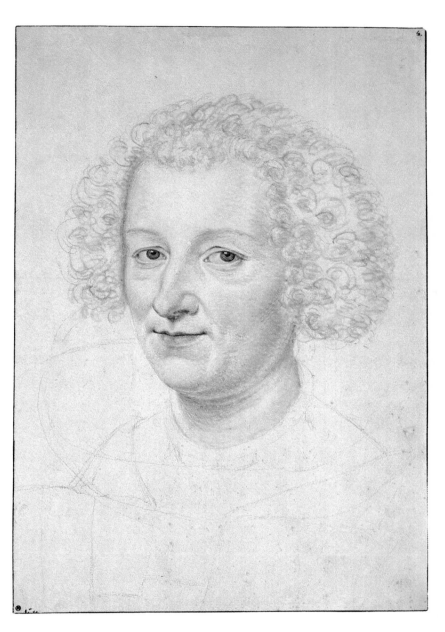

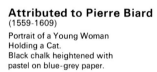

Attributed to Pierre Biard
(1559-1609)
Portrait of a Young Woman
Holding a Cat.
Black chalk heightened with
pastel on blue-grey paper.

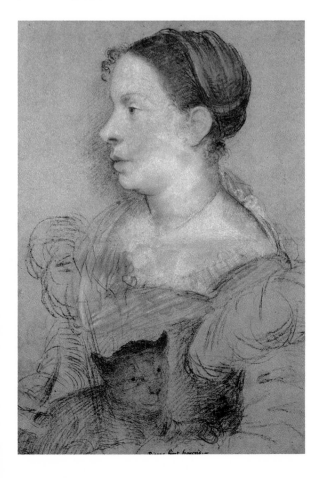

Daniel Dumonstier
(1574-1646)
Portrait of a Lady, c. 1630-1633.
Black chalk heightened with colours.

Pierre Biard, is a half-length in three-quarter view, with the face in profile. This pose continues the tradition begun by Leonardo da Vinci. The anecdotal element introduced by the cat is unusual for this early period, but steadily gained in importance in the centuries to come, reaching its height in the eighteenth century. The bluish grey paper contributes appreciably to the lifelike effect, adding to the relief and modelling. The use of coloured papers, in a wide range of hues, became increasingly frequent.

15

Beginning in the last quarter of the fifteenth century and continuing throughout the sixteenth, blue paper was the most popular with all the artists of the Venice region, where it was made and known as *carta azzurra* or *carta turchina*. It was later taken up by French and Dutch artists. Jacopo Bassano's *Head of an Apostle*, seen from the side as he gazes upwards, is an initial sketch for the figure in the left foreground of his painting *The Pentecost* of 1570 (Museo Civico, Bassano). The purpose of this pastel is comparable to that of a painted sketch, with the advantage of being more quickly done and giving, in a few thick strokes of charcoal and red chalk combined with pastel on blue paper, the essentials of the projected composition: attitude, lighting, colouring. The forthright strokes suggest the vigorous hand of a painter as much as a draughtsman; this is a trait peculiar to the Venetian artists.

Born at Urbino, in the Marches, Federico Barocci arrived at a synthesis of the leading masters of his time—Raphael, Michelangelo and Correggio. His own inventiveness comes out in three aspects of his work: in the expression; in a new sense of form achieved through shaded modelling, to which pastel was admirably suited; a new luminism created by lighting effects from below.

Barocci's pastels are rough sketches for details of his large figure compositions. In them he proves himself a master of colour and

Jacopo Bassano
(c. 1517-1592)

Head of an Apostle, c. 1570.
Charcoal, red chalk and
pastel on blue paper.

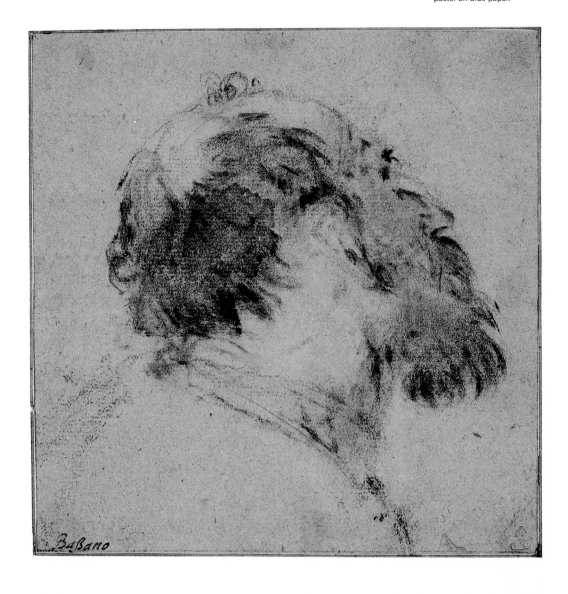

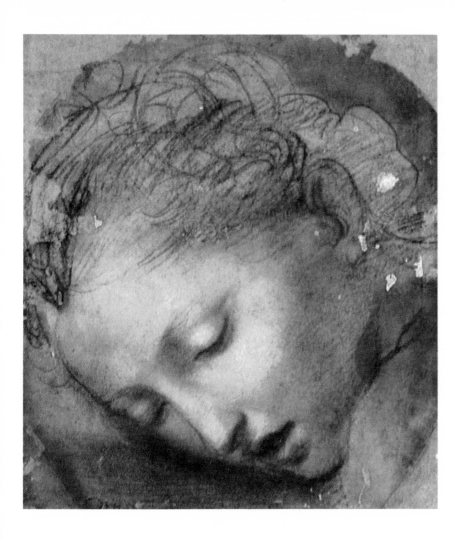

relief, contriving to enhance them by the effects of paper or card-board, which he generally chooses in tints of buff, grey or blue. The *Head of the Virgin* (black and red chalk heightened with pastel on grey paper) is a study for the woman supporting the Virgin in his *Deposition of Christ*, painted in 1568-1569 for the chapel of San Bernardino in Perugia Cathedral, where it still is. In the preparatory studies for this canvas, Barocci carefully worked out all the details of figures and draperies, using pastels of all colours. These pastel heads of his were destined to exert a shaping influence on several French artists of the eighteenth century, on Jean-Baptiste Deshays among others, who collected them and based his own studies on them. Several of Barocci's pastels were copied by François Lemoine, whose *Head of the Goddess Hebe* (see page 22) is undoubtedly derived from one of them.

The seventeenth-century Florentine artist Sebastiano Mazzoni, who worked mostly in Venice, has left a series of pastel studies remarkable for their dynamic forms and the wide range of colours employed. They are treated as if they were meant to be preparatory sketches, all the essential features being indicated: composition, movement, values, with colour laid in over black-chalk outlines. A strange luminism and an unusual polychromy are their specific characteristics.

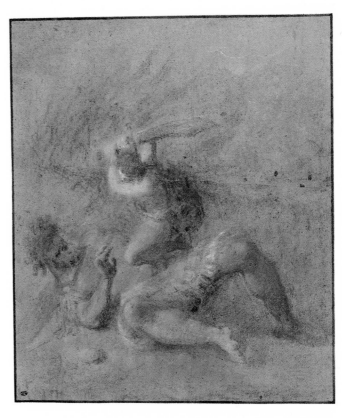

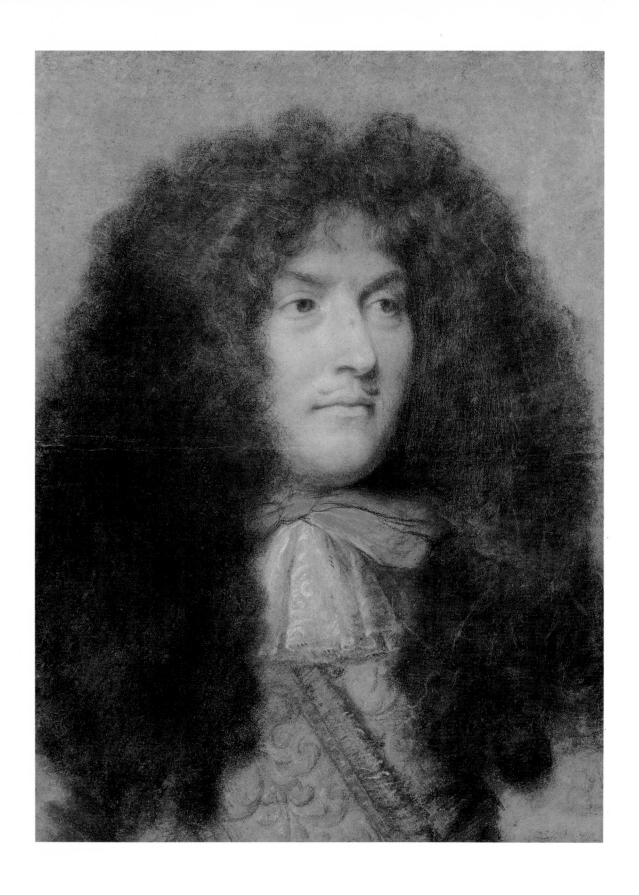

Charles Le Brun
(1619-1690)
Portrait of Louis XIV, c. 1665.
Pastel on grey-buff paper.

Joseph Vivien
(1657-1734)
Portrait of Louis de France,
Duc de Bourgogne, 1700.
Pastel.

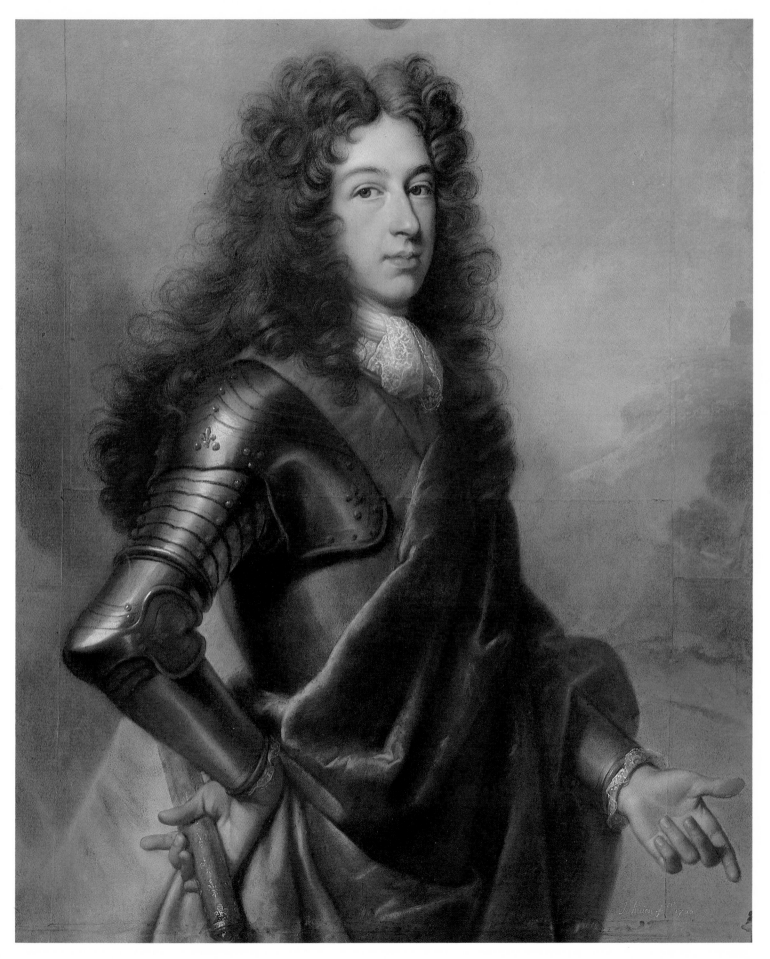

Charles Le Brun used pastel for his portraits of Louis XIV, which were done rapidly in front of the king, whom the artist represents with consummate mastery (c. 1665, Louvre, Paris). A gripping immediacy is achieved. The peruke and the coloured details of the costume are rendered economically, with a sure and sober hand. These direct, vigorously wrought studies were intended for one of the innumerable compositions illustrating the *Life of*

er, he stands very much on show, with a touch of pomp and stiffness.

Vivien made at least two versions of his portraits of the grandsons of Louis XIV; one of them is *Louis de France, Duc de Bourgogne* (see page 19). A set of three pastels made for the king is preserved in the Louvre; the other set of pastels (of smaller size but all signed and dated 1700) is now in the Munich museum;

Portraiture and decorative setting

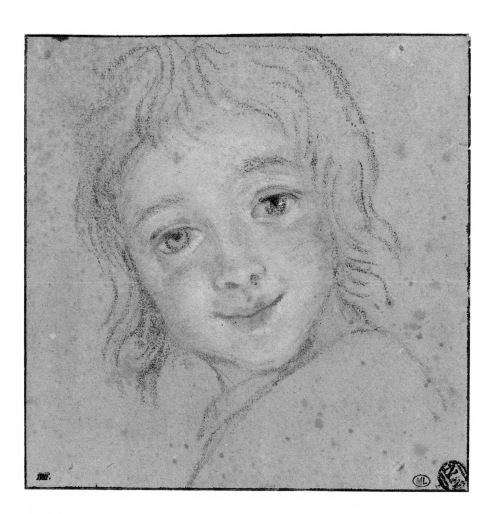

Antoine Coypel
(1661-1722)
Study of a Little Girl's Face.
Pastel on buff paper.

the King, some as paintings, as in the Galerie des Glaces at Versailles, others as tapestries. The study of the human face, and the feelings mirrored in it, was already a speciality of Le Brun, who in 1702 published his treatise *Méthode pour apprendre à dessiner les passions*.

In 1701 Joseph Vivien was admitted to the French Academy as a "Pastel Painter", on the strength of his portraits of *François Girardon, Sculptor* and *Robert de Cotte, Architect*. In these he created the prototype of the solemn, majestic, life-size portraits so much in demand in France throughout the eighteenth century. Vivien's pastels are built up with delicate strokes of shaded, blending colours. The reflection on armour and the shimmer of light on fabrics are rendered to perfection. This is an art of surface effects, and modelling is scarcely suggested. For Vivien the pastel was not merely an intermediary study: it was an end in itself, a complete and finished work, as large and imposing as an oil painting, whose effects he deliberately copied. The prolific eighteenth-century output of pastel portraits grew out of these examples, in which the sitter is generally shown in half-length, with his social or professional attributes; looking out at the view-

these latter were still in the Imperial Residence of Bavaria in 1729. This illustrates the multiplicity of these portrait commissions, executed in one or more copies for different members of a ruling family. Vivien exerted a dominant influence on several artists—on the Swede Gustav Lundberg and even on Maurice Quentin de La Tour in his early work. And Vivien's example was followed by Hyacinthe Rigaud, who also represented this transitional generation between the seventeenth and eighteenth century. Like Vivien, Rigaud emphasized the stately, theatrical aspect of his portraits, in which the sitters wear sumptuous costumes whose volume is amplified by broad draperies.

Antoine Coypel was one of the first to make the change of style that marks the transition from the seventeenth to the eighteenth century. His spontaneous studies of smiling children's faces were sketched out quickly with a few pastel strokes on a sheet of buff paper; they may have been used for his decorative compositions, perhaps one of the arches of the ceiling paintings he made, in Paris, Versailles and elsewhere, between 1700 and 1721; this would account for the very peculiar lighting, which rakes the faces from below.

François Lemoine emphasizes the ornamental aspect of his preparatory studies. After a thorough training in Paris, then in Italy, where he was most impressed by the grandiose decorative paintings of Lanfranco and Pietro da Cortona, Lemoine too specialized in ceiling decorations, on a monumental scale, painted with a broad, luminous sweep. His major achievement is the ceiling in the Salon d'Hercule at Versailles, completed in 1736,

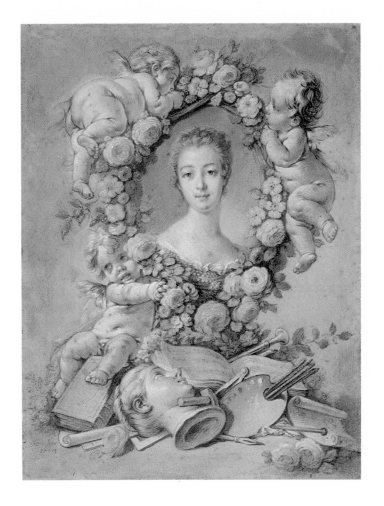

François Boucher
(1703-1770)

Madame de Pompadour, 1754.
Pastel on buff paper.

with figures in illusionist foreshortening, seen *da sotto in su*; his upturned heads were inspired by Barocci's pastels. Sketched with the ceiling of the Salon d'Hercule in mind, the *Head of the Goddess Hebe* (page 22), with flowers in her hair, is particularly successful in its engaging ease and grace. Lemoine makes the most of the blue paper and focuses the lighting on the smooth sweep of the neck and lower face.

François Boucher, as a pupil of Lemoine's, naturally treated similar themes, but with a heightened emphasis on decorative elements. Thus the head-and-shoulders portrait of *Madame de Pompadour*, of 1754, is surrounded by a garland of flowers held by three cherubs, while in the foreground below lie the attributes of the Arts. In the wide diversity of his subjects, ranging from history paintings and religious themes to *scènes galantes*, Boucher had a particular fondness for allegorical portraits, a genre which stemmed in part from the early examples painted by Rosalba Carriera. Here, as in the rest of his work, we find an unfailing elegance of composition, accurate lighting, a profusion of bright colours—pink, blue, yellow—and a flair for decoration which still exerts its florid charm.

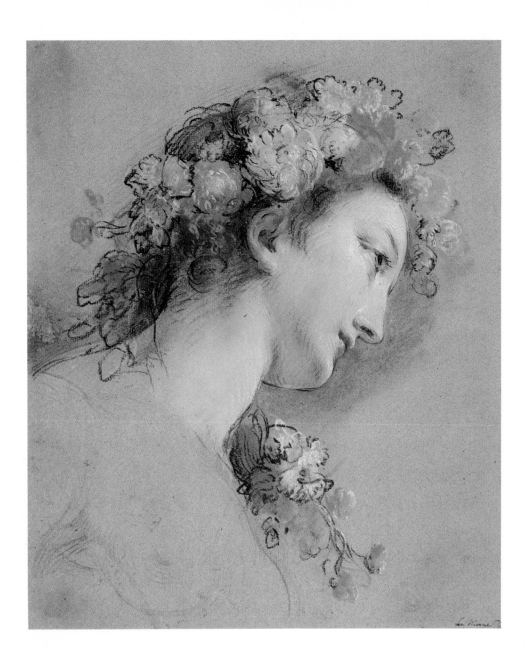

François Lemoine
(1688-1737)
Head of the Goddess Hebe, c. 1735.
Pastel on blue paper.

Rosalba Carriera
(1675-1757)
Enrichetta Anna Sofia
di Modena (detail), 1723.
Pastel on cardboard.

The Venetian artist Rosalba Carriera made a genuine innovation when she turned to pastel as the essential medium of her Italian society portraits. Her success was such that she went to Paris in 1720, at the invitation of the French banker and collector Pierre Crozat: she received an enthusiastic welcome and lived in a circle of Parisian artists and collectors from April 1720 to March 1721, becoming friendly with Watteau and the print dealer Pierre Jean Mariette.

The bulk of Rosalba Carriera's work consists of portraits of women. In addition to her superb mastery of the pastel technique, she had a distinctive approach of her own: a more graceful conception of portraiture, in which nudity could be justified by the allegorical content; a desire to appeal to the eye by certain devices, such as flowers in the hair and low-necked dresses; and a subdued palette of pinks, blues and whites. With her, for the first time, we find an aesthetic preoccupation, a discreet emphasis on grace and seductiveness, which from now on, throughout the eighteenth century, became one of the keynotes of pastel painting.

The novelty lay in her use of unusually mellow colours, applied in broad flat areas, with a velvety, vaporous texture, and subtly harmonizing and re-echoing each other. The drawing and structure are firm and accurate. Eyelids and nose were often laid in beforehand with a stroke of red chalk or red pastel; then the outlines were skilfully shaded off, so that the resulting forms were not only well enveloped but solidly structured. The soundness of the preparatory work is concealed by the outward lightness of the figure, which conduces to an idealized effect, casting an aura of mystery and unreality over the sitter.

Rosalba Carriera always works with dry pastel sticks, with a lavish use of the shading stump, a technique which made reworking easy; she was especially fond of light-toned colours. Technical experiment interested her and she freely answered the questions put to her in 1719 by her friend Casotti regarding the use of gum as a vehicle or binder of colours: "Special artists do not bind pastels with gum, but with tailor's chalk and ground shells." And she added further on that, while she had tried the pastels made in Flanders and Rome, those of Paris seemed to her the best of all. Elsewhere she touches on the limits of the technical issue: "I should have much to say about pastel, but I know well enough

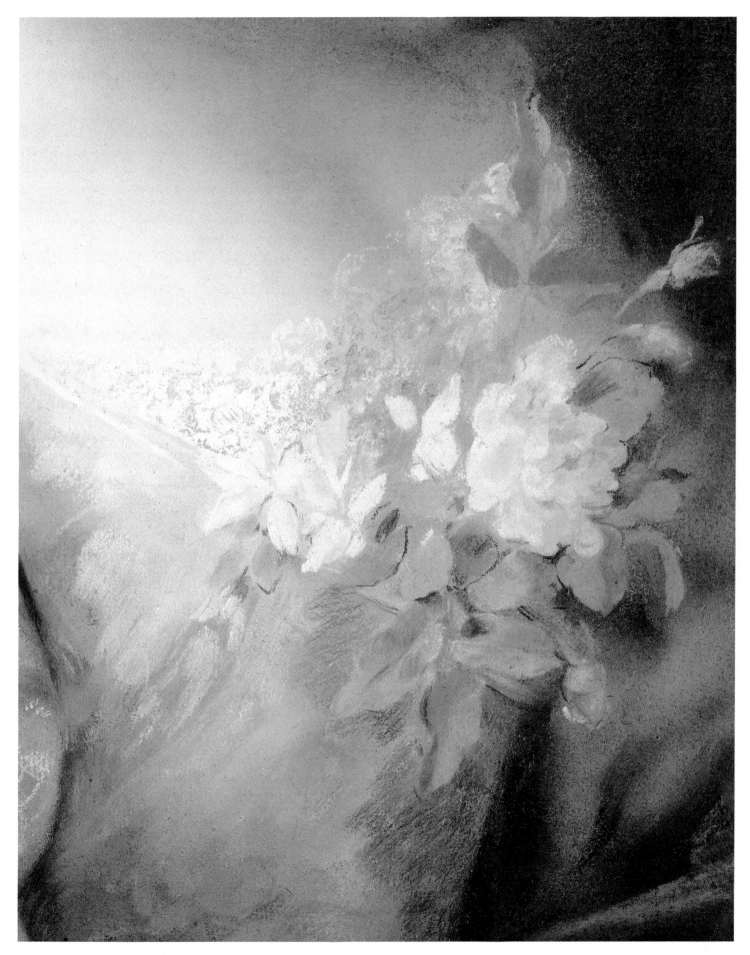

that the success of a work depends on something more than the artist's crayons or paper. Studio recipes provide some good indications for painters, but the material side of the work is only a secondary matter'' (Giovanni Vianelli, quoted in *Journal de Rosalba Carriera pendant son séjour à Paris en 1720 et 1721*, edited by Alfred Sensier, Paris, 1865). According to this diary-chronicle, she executed about fifty portraits during her stay in Paris; the

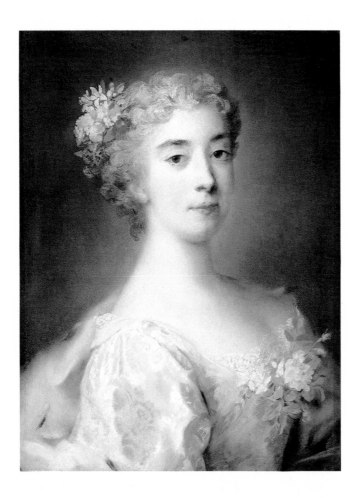

Rosalba Carriera
(1675-1757)
Enrichetta Anna Sofia
di Modena, 1723.
Pastel on cardboard.

great bulk of her pastels were done after her return to Venice, in addition to a few oil paintings and miniatures. During a visit to Modena in 1723 she painted the portrait of *Enrichetta Anna Sofia di Modena*, one of the three daughters of the reigning duke, Rinaldo d'Este. The purpose of these portraits, executed in several versions, was to make the princesses known to prospective husbands.

It was in Venice, where the intellectual and social role of women was then fully recognized, that Rosalba painted her *Portrait of Caterina Barbarigo*, one of the outstanding figures of the Venetian intelligentsia: this likeness of a brilliant, self-reliant woman reflects a whole age of plenitude and maturity. In both portraits we find the same haughty grace, due to the position of the head, thrown back with an air of pride.

The influence of Rosalba Carriera is evident in the evolution of female portraiture, a genre much in favour throughout the eighteenth century, in the hands of such Parisian artists as Nattier, Vigée-Lebrun, Lemoine and also Boucher, to mention only a few examples. Towards mid-century, the portrait of a woman began serving as a pretext for the introduction of mythological subjects and so merged with history painting.

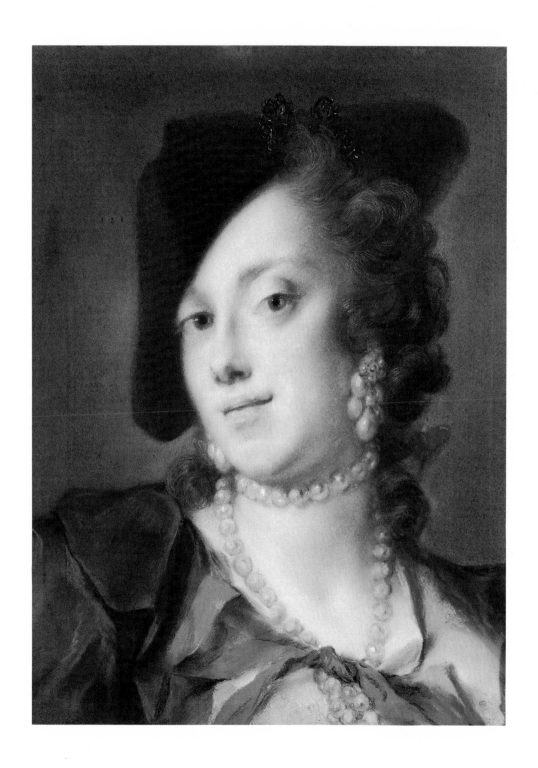

Rosalba Carriera
(1675-1757)

Portrait of Caterina Barbarigo.
Pastel on cardboard.

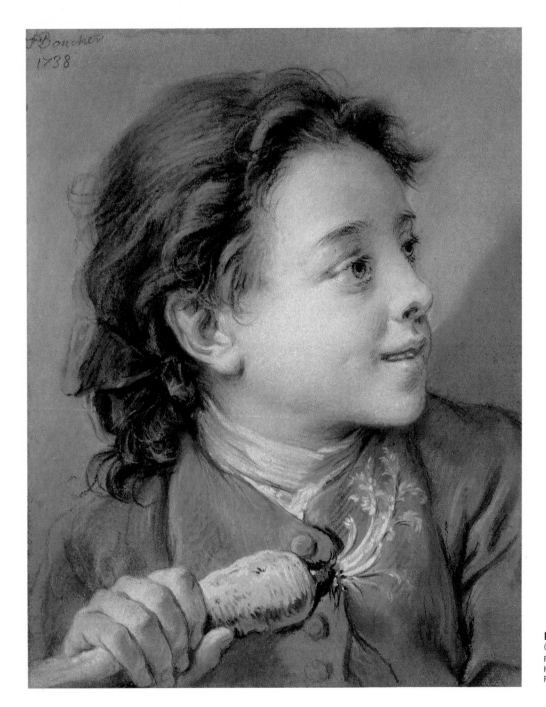

François Boucher
(1703-1770)
Portrait of a Young Man
Holding a Carrot, 1738.
Pastel.

Almost all the French pastellists of the mid-eighteenth century helped to define this playful, appealing, spontaneous style, as we find it illustrated here in François Boucher and Jean-Baptiste Perronneau. It is seen at its best in portraits of smiling, mischievous children and adolescents sketched from the life. In both examples the figure is shown in bust length, cut off in such a way that only one hand is visible. The shoulders are in front view, the head in profile, the better to suggest mobility, in accordance with a stock device of portrait painters. The colour scheme, all in bright, delicate, translucent hues, with soft, plastic modelling for the face of the *Girl with a Cat*, sets off the velvety texture of the handling, for this portrait is executed on vellum in an unusual combination of colours—greens and blues. Perronneau is primarily a colourist, aiming at uncommon harmonies in most of his pastels; for example, garnet and violet set off by a yellow ground.

He was one of the first, as early as 1747, even before Chardin, to render shading by green hatchings, a wholly new departure; it can be seen here in the strokes running along the neck of the young girl (identified as the daughter of the engraver Gabriel Huquier). This tender response to childhood is common to many eighteenth-century artists, such as Watteau, Van Loo, Chardin, Greuze. It was new in French portrait painting, and becomes even more marked in the nineteenth century.

Comparing Perronneau's style with that of La Tour (for they were rivals), one detects in it a more spirited execution, a deliberate cultivation of relief in the texture, a more evident suppleness and freedom of handling. Perronneau made his mark as a pastel painter from 1745 on, while continuing to paint in oils. Not so with Boucher: he is a fine and important pastellist, but his work as a whole is centred on oil painting and decoration.

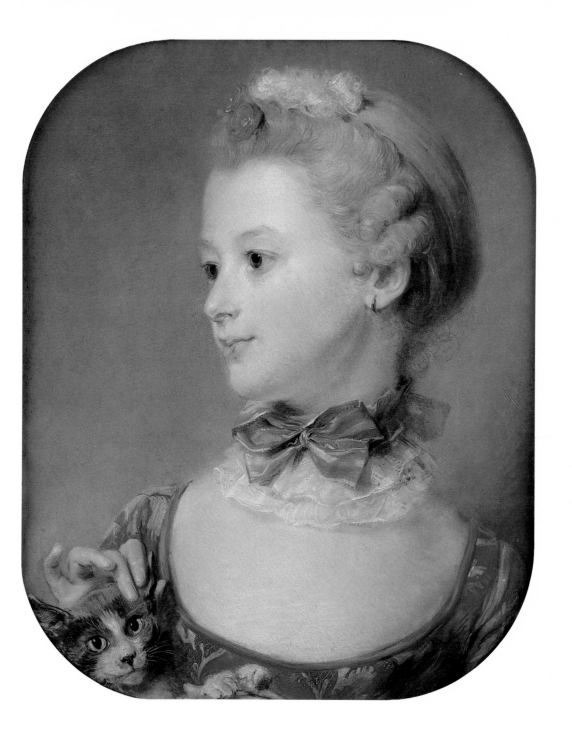

Jean-Baptiste Perronneau
(1715-1783)

Portrait of a Girl
with a Cat, 1747.
Pastel on vellum.

Pastels were brought into fashion in Paris in 1720 by Rosalba Carriera, and it was her success that prompted Maurice Quentin de La Tour to take up this technique. (His copy of Rosalba's *Nymph of Apollo's Retinue* is in the Musée Lécuyer at Saint-Quentin.) Received into the Academy in 1746, La Tour was promoted to the rank of councillor in 1751. In 1782 he founded a drawing school in his native town of Saint-Quentin in Picardy. Reacting against the stately portraits of Rigaud and Vivien, and against the mythological settings of Lemoine and Nattier, La Tour reverted to a more realistic and sober approach. He used pastel exclusively; not a single oil painting by his hand is known to exist. As portraitist to the royal family of France, he also did many likenesses of high-ranking courtiers. His abiding purpose was to convey the temperament and psychology of his sitter by the expression of the face, to record a feeling he sensed, a fleet-ing emotion. "Unknown to them, I descend into the depths of my sitters and I bring back the whole man," was La Tour's comment on his method. Beginning with several preparatory studies, he concentrated chiefly on the smile and gaze. The initial study was done in black chalk, heightened with white. The second study was devoted to the oval of the face, and from this basis he sometimes went on to do an overall sketch of the sitter before embarking on the final portrait. In the case of official portraits of court personages, La Tour began with a rapid sketch from life of the sitter's head on a circular sheet of paper, which he then pasted onto the overall composition in his studio. The Goncourts already, in their study of La Tour, commented on the number of these "preparations" made for a single portrait: often as many as four or five in black crayon and chalk, in red chalk and coloured crayons, before tackling the pastel.

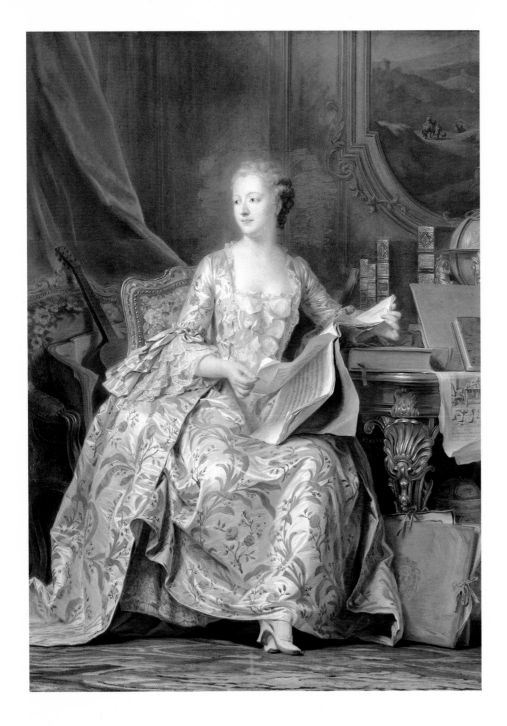

Maurice Quentin de La Tour
(1704-1788)

Portrait of Madame de
Pompadour, 1752-1755.
Pastel on blue-grey paper.

Portrait of Gabriel-Bernard
de Rieux, 1741.
Pastel.

Of monumental dimensions, this pastel of *Gabriel-Bernard de Rieux* was exhibited at the Salon of 1741 (No. 118). As president of the Parlement de Paris, Rieux is sitting in his office, wearing a black robe and red mantle, with an open book on his lap; under his feet is a Turkey carpet; behind him, protecting him from a draught, is a folding screen. The decor on the left may be that of the drawing room in the Château de Glisolles (Eure), owned by the Rieux family. The globe is similar to the one in La Tour's large portrait of *Madame de Pompadour*.

For the famous pastel of *Madame de Pompadour*, commissioned from La Tour in 1751, begun in 1752 and exhibited at the Salon of 1755 (No. 58), also of monumental dimensions, only the head was executed from life; it was done, according to his wont, on a separate sheet of paper (whose irregular edges are visible in a raking light) which was then pasted onto the full-length portrait,

which itself was made up of several sheets of paper assembled and pasted together. The king's favourite is surrounded by various objects symbolizing literature, music, astronomy and engraving, and evoking her role as a patroness of the arts. Madame de Pompadour herself had been given lessons by Boucher and made some etchings and line engravings of her own; the print visible on the right of the pastel bears the mention *Pompadour sculpsit*.

These two portraits by La Tour are magnificent and consummate achievements. As a technical feat they are unsurpassed, with the flawless rendering of the figures in their characteristic attitude and "native" setting, and a texture so finely diversified that it suggests to perfection all the different materials represented, silks, velvets, brocades, carpets, lace, woodwork and so on, without detracting from the serene amplitude of the whole.

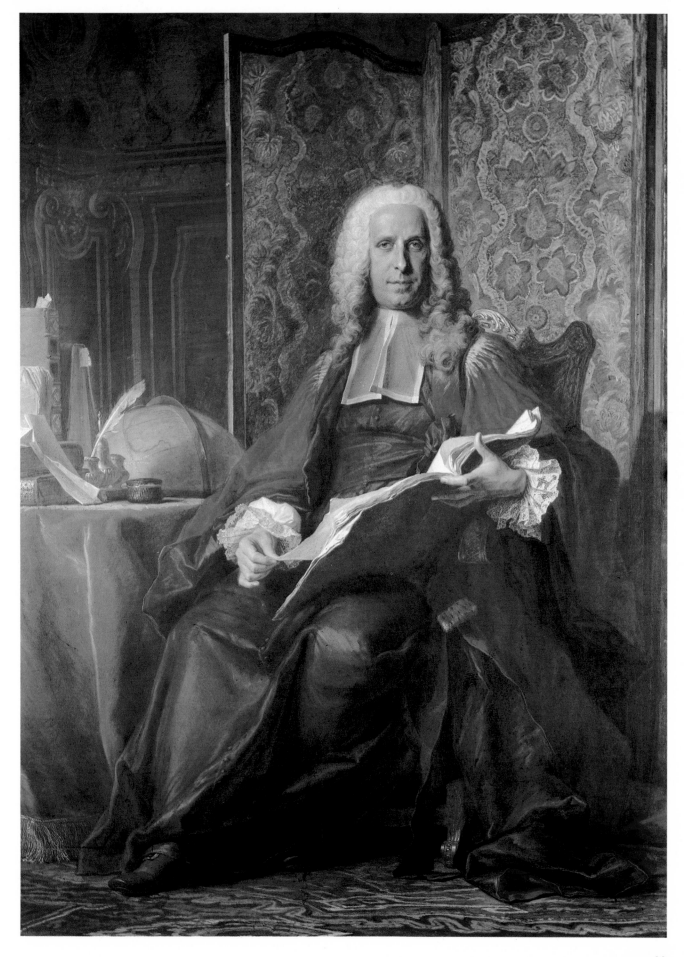

As a tribute of admiration and friendship, the pastels portraying artists are often particularly attractive, counting among the most refined and elegant works of the eighteenth century. The *Portrait of the Painter Charles Natoire* was in 1741 one of the two reception pieces presented to the Académie Royale de Peinture in Paris by the Swedish artist Gustav Lundberg, whose admittance to the Academy required a certificate of exemption since he was

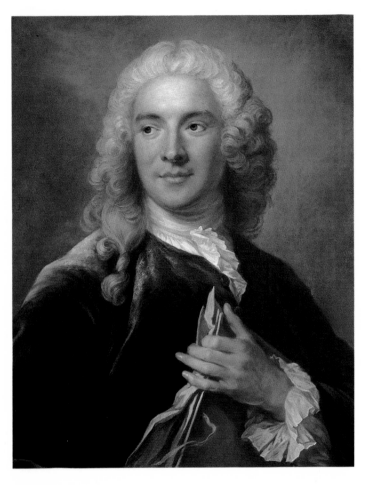

Gustav Lundberg
(1695-1786)
Portrait of the Painter
Charles Natoire, c. 1741.
Pastel on blue paper.

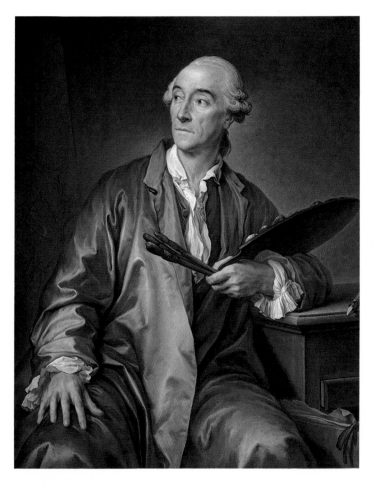

Alexis III Loir
(1712-1785)
Portrait of the Painter
Clément Belle, c. 1779.
Pastel on copper.

a Protestant. Lundberg had been in France since 1717 and probably received advice or lessons from Rosalba Carriera when she was in Paris in 1720-1721. Several of his court portraits, in particular those of Louis XV and Marie Leszczynska of about 1740, are in the Versailles museum. The painter Charles Natoire is portrayed here against a neutral background, devoid of any setting, in a sober, easy pose—face in front view, bust in three-quarter view, a slight emphasis laid on the gesture of the hand. The pastel strokes are clearly visible, less blended and shaded than in Vivien; the modelling is more accentuated, the relief effect sharper, than in Rosalba Carriera. The texture is velvety and chalky; the monochrome of dark grey, light grey and white is faintly heightened with blue.

The *Portrait of the Painter Clément Belle* by Alexis III Loir, a history painter and professor at the Académie Royale, was also a reception piece at the Academy, in 1779. Life-size, it is painted

on copper, and this unusual ground gives the modelling a peculiar finesse and brilliance. The shades of pink used for the long satin coat worn by the sitter are equally uncommon. Belle is represented in his studio, pausing for a moment from his work, still holding his palette and brushes, but keeping the pose in front view, with averted face as he glances off to the left.

From the early eighteenth century, the self-portrait was a theme that increasingly attracted artists in France, for it gave them an opportunity of recording the change now coming over their social standing and the image of their new status. They liked to show themselves in their studio in town clothes, with a powdered wig. In Joseph Boze's *Self-Portrait* one notes the keen gaze directed straight at the spectator and the unflinching naturalism which led the artist to include even the skin disease marking his face. Remarkable here are the high quality of the execution, the sureness of touch, the fine colour scheme of grey, blue and green: the result is an intense and arresting presence. The grey satin costume is beautifully rendered with all its reflections; its smooth surface contrasts most effectively with the uneven, pock-marked skin of the face. As court painter, from 1785, to Louis XVI and Marie-Antoinette, Boze got into trouble after the Revolution and spent some months in prison in 1793.

When La Tour and Chardin, who stand out as the finest French

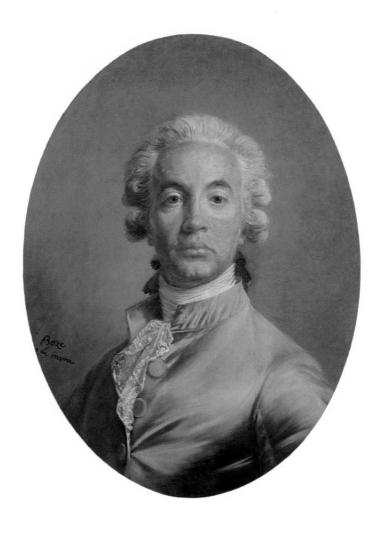

Joseph Boze
(1745-1826)
Self-Portrait.
Pastel on blue paper.

pastellists of the eighteenth century, paint their own portrait, they seem to lay bare the very essence of their style and personality. This theme, touching home and concerning none but themselves, called forth the full powers of their invention and research. La Tour, doing what he could not allow himself to do with anyone else, focused entirely on the oval of his face, treating it like a mask, isolated from any context (hair, clothes, setting). Its contours are conjured up with a few emphatic strokes, shaded with white or pink to give the lights, the shadows then being laid in with parallel hatchings. This *Self-Portrait* is connected with the *Self-Portrait with a Hat* exhibited at the Salon of 1742 (No. 131). It conveys a keen sense of life and communicates the engaging irony of his sharp-eyed glance, accompanied by a symbolic smile. The ''mask-like'' effect, which the Goncourt brothers saw in it, seems an accurate description of the underlying uneasiness one feels in La Tour, an artist who tried in vain to create the image of the happy man he would have liked to be.

Chardin turned to pastel in the later years of his career, when his eyesight was beginning to fail. "My infirmities have prevented me from continuing to paint in oils, and I have fallen back on pastels," he wrote in 1778 to the Comte d'Angiviller, Superintendent of Royal Buildings. In his self-portraits Chardin comes before us with a simplicity and modesty wholly at variance with the traditional style. No pose, no attitude: here is the artist in his

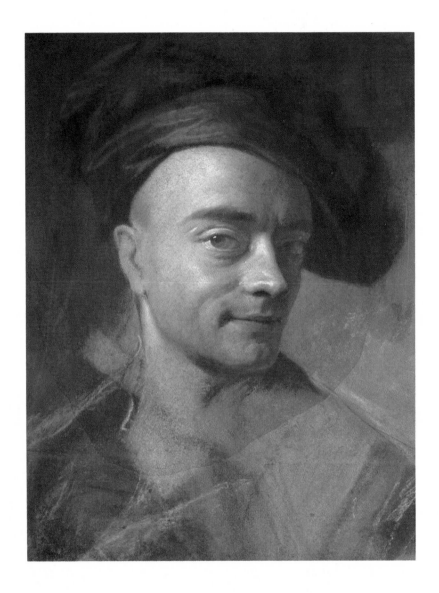

Maurice Quentin de La Tour
(1704-1788)
Self-Portrait with a Hat, c. 1742.
Pastel.

Jean-Baptiste-Siméon Chardin
(1699-1779)
Self-Portrait with Spectacles, 1771.
Pastel on grey-blue paper.

studio, in working garb, with no wig, wearing his spectacles, his headcloth held in place by a knotted blue ribbon. More than any other French artist of his time, he expresses the dignity and simplicity of the individual human being.

Two of Chardin's innovations were momentous. One was his system of parallel hatchings of pure colour which determine the modelling and render form, relief and light simultaneously. The other was his thick texture of superimposed layers of colour recalling his handling of the oil paints, by a building up of successive layers for the purpose of obtaining the utmost perfection in the structure, tonalities and grain of the paintwork. He conceived the idea of leaving his broad hatchings plainly visible by superimposing them and criss-crossing them; in other words, he deliberately emphasized texture and paintwork at the expense of contours, which up to then had been given priority in accor-

dance with academic tradition. Here Chardin gives a foretaste of the innovations to come a century later with the divided brushstroke. With him one line of development of the portrait reaches fulfilment—the portrait focused on the face in close-up. With him it becomes a complete presence, both physical and existential. Chardin employed pastel boldly, crushing the powdery stick against the paper and patterning it with streaks which harmonize with the whole when seen from a distance. This technique of separate strokes was revolutionary at the time. In the Louvre are three self-portraits by Chardin. In the one reproduced here, he breaks away challengingly from pure realism when he renders the blurred effect in the part of the face which is seen through the distorting lens of the spectacles. Against the ground of blue-grey paper re-echoed in the areas of blue, green and brown, the face is built up in browns and pinks with blue and green shading.

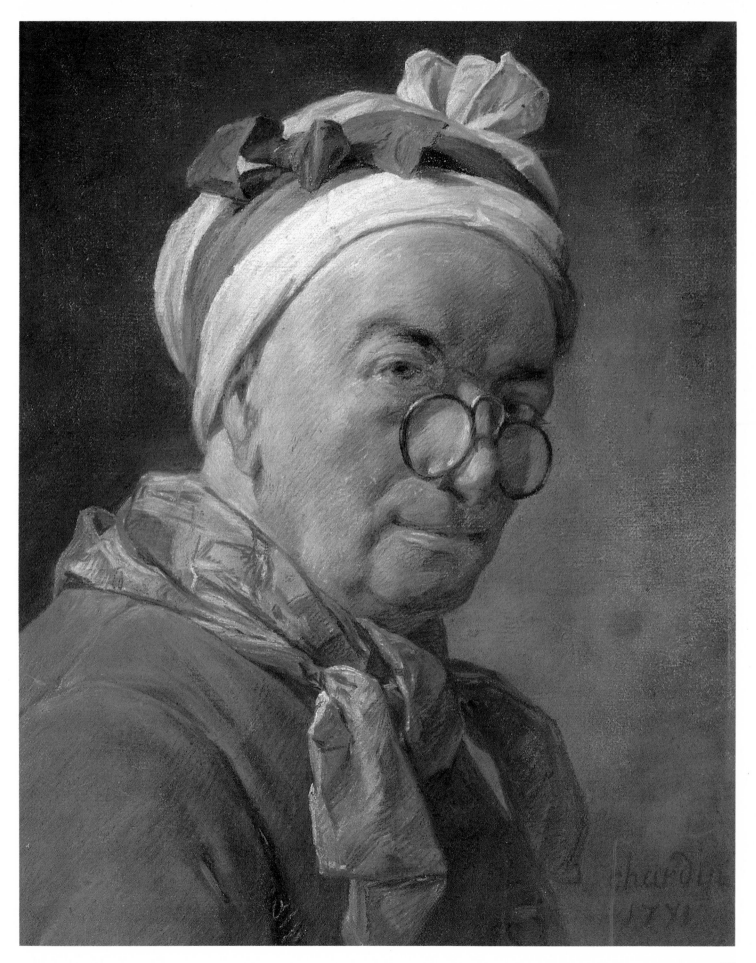

33

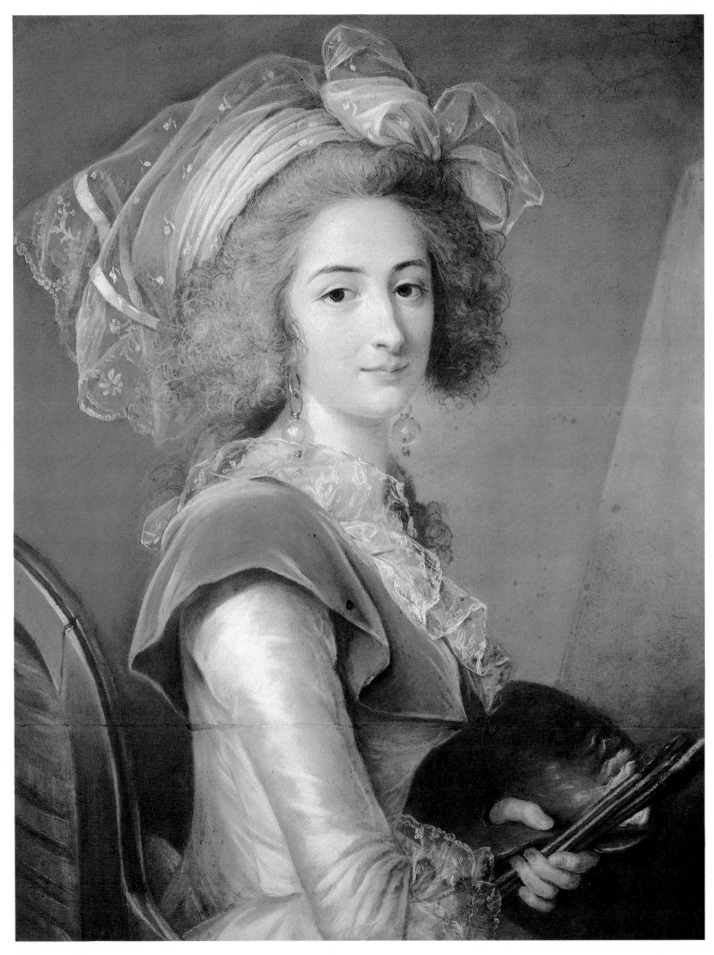

34

During the eighteenth century several women artists followed up the path opened by Rosalba Carriera by practising simultaneously pastel, miniature painting and oil painting. Among the best known and most active were Theresa Concordia Mengs, Marie-Suzanne Roslin, Adélaïde Labille-Guiard, Elisabeth Vigée-Lebrun, Marie-Gabrielle Capet, and Madeleine-Françoise Basseporte. Most of them were born into a family of artists and

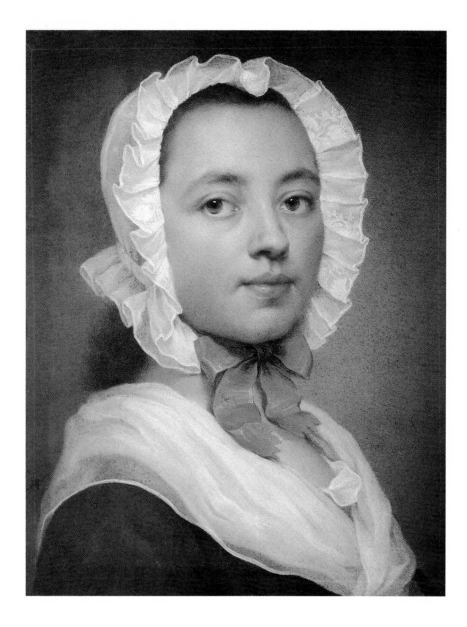

Adélaïde Labille-Guiard
(1749-1803)
Self-Portrait with Easel
and Palette, 1782.
Pastel on blue paper.

Theresa Concordia Mengs
(1725-1806)
Portrait of the Artist's
Sister Julia Mengs, c. 1750.
Pastel on paper.

several of them married painters. Theresa Concordia Mengs, for example, was the sister of the painter Anton Raphael Mengs and, what was unusual at that time, received the same schooling that he did; she settled in Rome in the 1740s and there, in 1765, she and her husband, the painter Anton von Maron, became members of the Accademia di San Luca—the academy of painting. The *Portrait of the Artist's Sister Julia Mengs* compels attention by its simplicity, forthrightness and realism. The careful, minutely detailed technique announces Neo-Classicism.

Adélaïde Labille-Guiard portrayed herself in pastel in front of her studio easel, holding her oil painter's palette and brushes, thus hinting at the multiplicity of her talents. Signed and dated 1782,

this pastel was exhibited at the Salon of that year. She is fashionably dressed in white satin, blue velvet and white lace, with an elaborate cap of embroidered voile knotted at one side. After studying pastel with La Tour for about five years, Labille-Guiard developed a taste for a rather sophisticated *mise en scène*, at once theatrical and intimist. In 1782 she applied for admittance to the Academy, where she was received the following year as a portrait painter. From 1774, her work was often compared with that of Elisabeth Vigée-Lebrun, who was six years younger. From that date, they both exhibited regularly at the Salon, then at the Salon de la Correspondance. Labille-Guiard kept largely to pastel, while Vigée-Lebrun preferred oil painting.

*"The smoothness of fine skin, the gloss
and transparency of bodies, the colouring
of flowers, the down and bloom of fruit..."*

Liotard

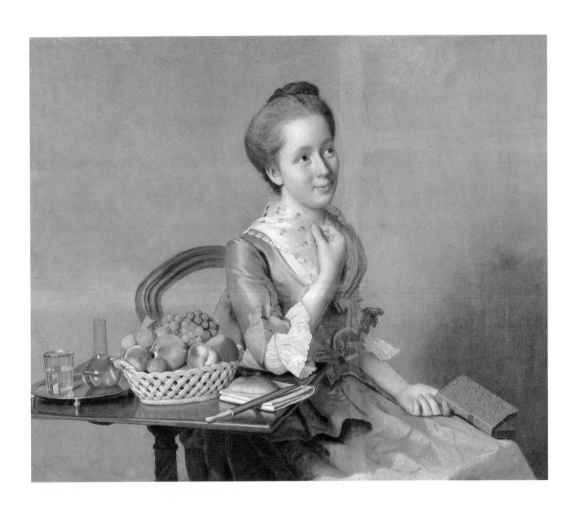

Jean-Etienne Liotard
(1702-1789)
Portrait of Madame
Necker, 1761.
Pastel on canvas.

Supposed Portrait of the
Countess of Coventry, 1749.
Pastel on vellum.

The *Supposed Portrait of the Countess of Coventry* was executed by Jean-Etienne Liotard in at least three versions, with variants in the face, colour scheme and accessories (letters lying on the Turkey carpet, with or without a vase of flowers, the star-patterned cushion, etc.). In all three we have the same Oriental costume, with which the artist could have dressed several different sitters. In the pastel version in the Geneva museum, reproduced here, Liotard is probably using the lay-out, setting and figure pose of a portrait painted several years earlier, with the change of certain details. This would seem to account for the subtle interplay between two distinct sitters, one a dark-haired girl named Mimica in the Amsterdam and Geneva versions, the other the fair-haired Mary Gunning (later Countess of Coventry) in the Swallowfield version. The colouring of the Geneva pastel keeps to a much brighter scheme of whites, reds, blues and a few touches of green and yellow.

In 1761 Liotard painted his *Portrait of Madame Necker*, née Suzanne Curchod, to whom Gibbon had been engaged a few years before, who became the mother of the future Madame de Staël and at this time had a well-known literary salon in Geneva. Liotard took this portrait with him to Vienna, where the Empress

Maria Theresa bought it in 1762 without knowing the sitter's identity. The painter then regretted selling it and obtained permission from the empress to make a copy of it. Using a neutral ground without accessories, he centres the composition on the smiling, upward-glancing sitter, who has paused for a moment in her reading and is about to turn to the collation on the table. It forms a soberly composed still life: a platter with glass and decanter, a basket of fruit, a knife and folded napkin. Some twenty years later Liotard disregarded the usual rules of perspective when he again drew some fruit, pears, figs and plums, with a roll and a similarly placed knife on a chiffonnier on which he wrote in red pastel: "painted by J.E. Liotard at the age of 80." He refers to it in a letter to his elder son (24 September 1782): "In the past month and a half I have painted four fruit pictures... These four pictures are fresher and livelier, and the objects are more detached and forthcoming, with more relief and lifelikeness, than those of Van Huysum, but they are not so well finished. When I was only thirty, I could not have done them so well, having more skill now than I had then. They have been thought so fine that I have been asked to add my name and age of eighty years."

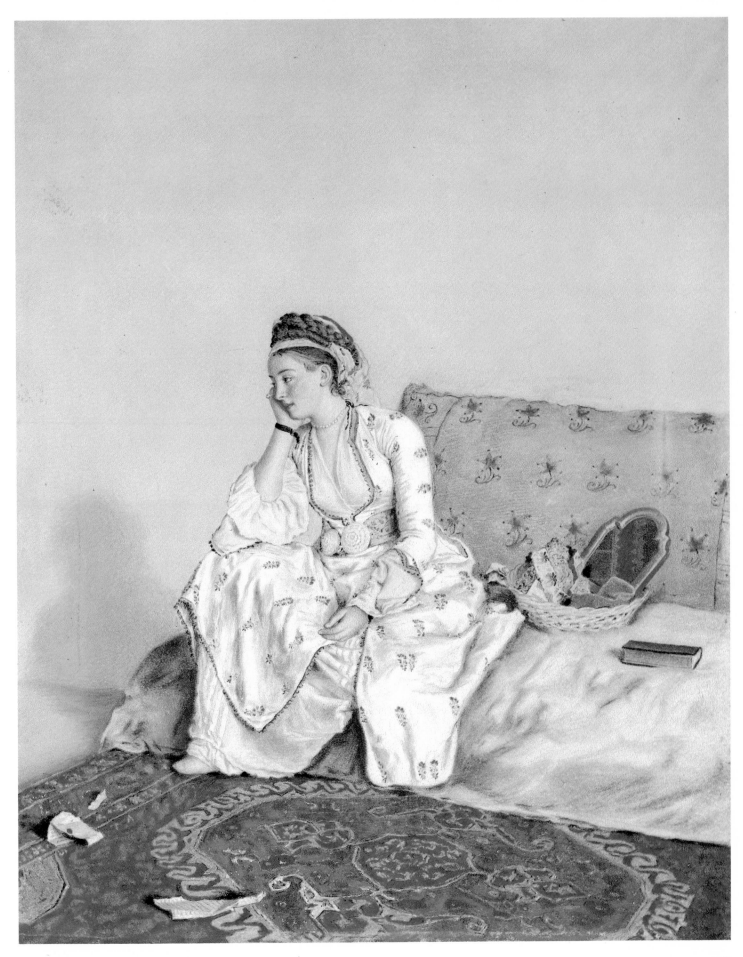

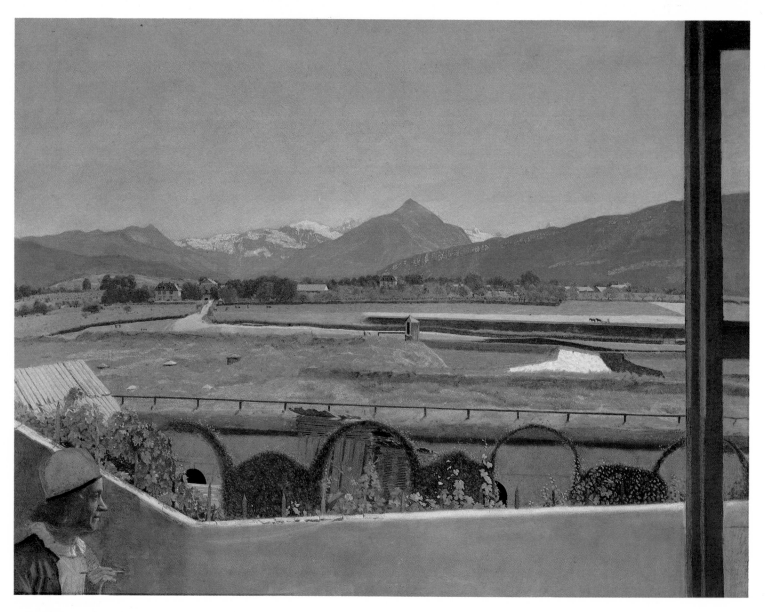

Jean-Etienne Liotard
(1702-1789)
View of Geneva from the Artist's
House with Self-Portrait, c. 1765-1770.
Pastel and gouache on vellum.

The space of this Liotard still life is constructed in such a way that the spectator has the impression of seeing the level top on which the fruit lies as if it had been uptilted on a vertical plane. By a distortion of the picture plane, giving the effect of a sharp incline, the artist contrives to give a more synthetic view of the objects. This device was a novelty at the time, in 1782; it was employed a century later in Cézanne's still lifes. The half-open drawer, a device already used by Chardin, adds a further effect of relief in the foreground. But in Chardin the picture space is built up in traditional linear perspective with a central vanishing point. Chardin often used a diagonal line, in the shape of a knife handle or a flower stalk, to break up the horizontal plane of a table placed in the foreground. Liotard here does not use the diagonal for this purpose, but rather to balance the composition and fill out the right side. A pattern of re-echoing colours catches and holds the spectator's eye, which perceives these colour areas along inter-secting trajectories: the accord between the purplish blue plums and the blue cloth sticking out of the drawer, between the alter-nating greens of the figs to right and left, heightened by the reddish brown tone, runs along a diagonal trajectory starting from the left side of the picture. Liotard connects the colours together by an abstract geometric pattern, while Chardin connected forms and colours by the impinging light that modified the shadings on objects.

The only landscape Liotard ever painted, this *View of Geneva from the Artist's House* might equally well be entitled "Self-Portrait against a Landscape." Executed about 1765-1770 in pastel and gouache on vellum, it shows the countryside beyond the Saint-Antoine quarter and the mountains of Savoy, with the Mont-Blanc massif in the distance. The bust figure of the artist on the lower left, in profile, has the precision of a Quattrocento portrait, with the same cool light impinging sharply on a terrace overlooking open country or through half-open windows with a boundless prospect. The vellum ground amplifies the comparison with the fifteenth century and the exacting art of illumination.

Jean-Etienne Liotard
(1702-1789)
Still Life with Fruit, Roll
and Knife, 1782.
Pastel on vellum.

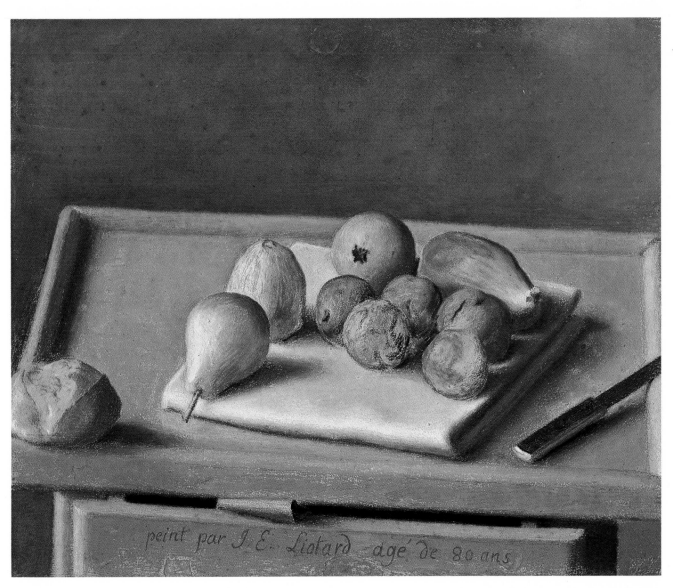

The artifice of a new sensibility

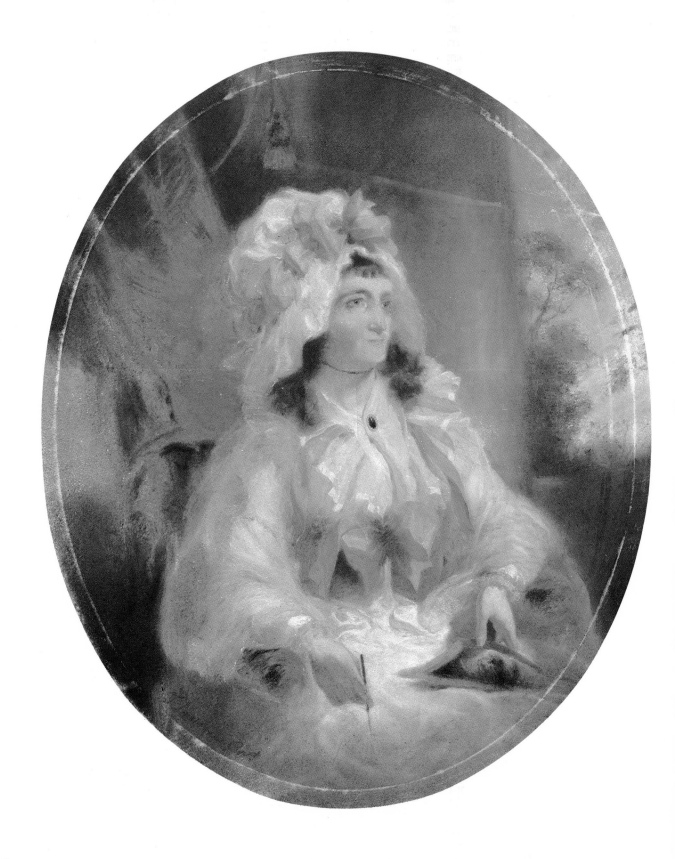

Sir Thomas Lawrence
(1769-1830)
Portrait of Miss Mary Hartley, c. 1790.
Pastel.

40

The coming of a new mood and climate towards the end of the eighteenth century, prefiguring Romanticism and even pre-Impressionism, is heralded in certain portraits, like the *Little Girl with Cherries* by the English pastellist John Russell, who posed his figures out of doors against a background of leafage and open sky. This is in marked contrast with the pastel portraits illustrated up to this point, which were mostly placed in a closed

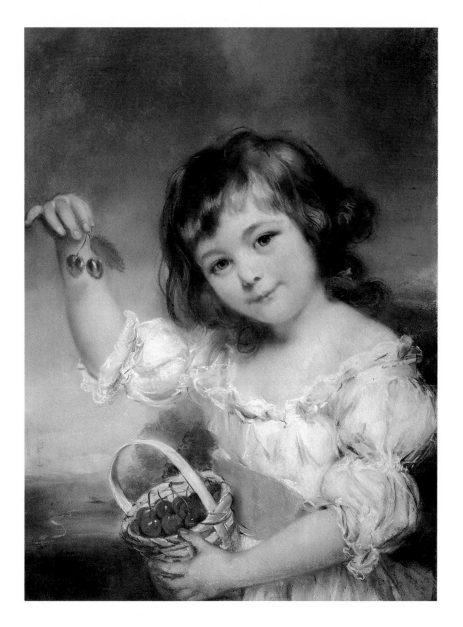

John Russell
(1745-1806)
Little Girl with Cherries.
Pastel on paper.

setting of boudoir, drawing room or studio, or else were shown against a neutral background. Something has also changed in the attitude of the figure, which is now seen in motion, rather in the manner of a snapshot. Russell's little girl looks smilingly at the spectator and seems to be offering him the cherries held in her hand.

Portraits of women and playing children are apt to be posed now against a landscape background. This new pre-Romantic feeling for nature appears first of all in English painting, and from there, through the influence of Thomas Lawrence, Copley Fielding and Richard Parkes Bonington, it spread to France and marked the early work of Delacroix and Géricault.

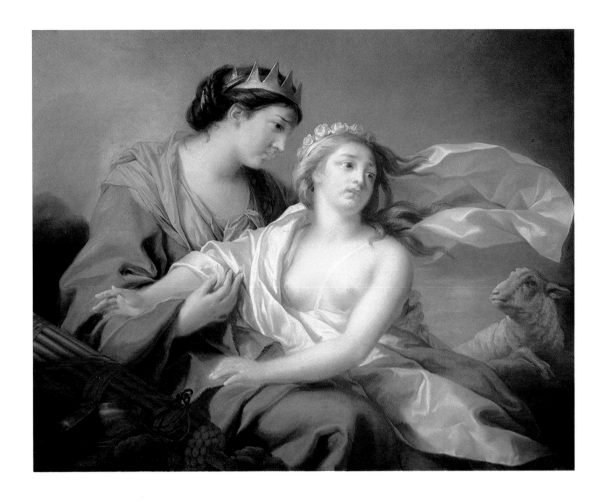

Elisabeth Vigée-Lebrun
(1755-1842)
Innocence Taking Refuge in
the Arms of Justice.
Pastel.

At this crossroads-point of the late eighteenth century, several streams of influence coalesce in this rather theatrical allegory of *Innocence Taking Refuge in the Arms of Justice*. In it too appears a new pre-Neoclassical accent. Elisabeth Vigée-Lebrun had studied the Greco-Roman Renaissance and the historical compositions of David, and from them, for this early work, she may have taken certain elements of stylization.

The pastel by Prud'hon, *Bust of a Young Woman Wearing a Diadem*, symbolizes the transition from graceful eighteenth-century allegory to the stricter Neoclassical revival of antique art at the beginning of the nineteenth century. An outstanding work, this pastel combines all the qualities of drawing, modelling and colour. It served as a preliminary study for the allegorical figure of Fortune on the right side of a picture entitled *The Scorn of Riches*, which was painted by Prud'hon's pupil Constance Mayer on the basis of sketches made by the master. Signed and dated 1804, the oil painting is now in the Hermitage Museum in Leningrad. This elaborate pastel study, almost a complete work in its own right, was also executed on canvas. The strong profile emphasizes the bas-relief effect of the fully modelled figure, obviously inspired by antique models.

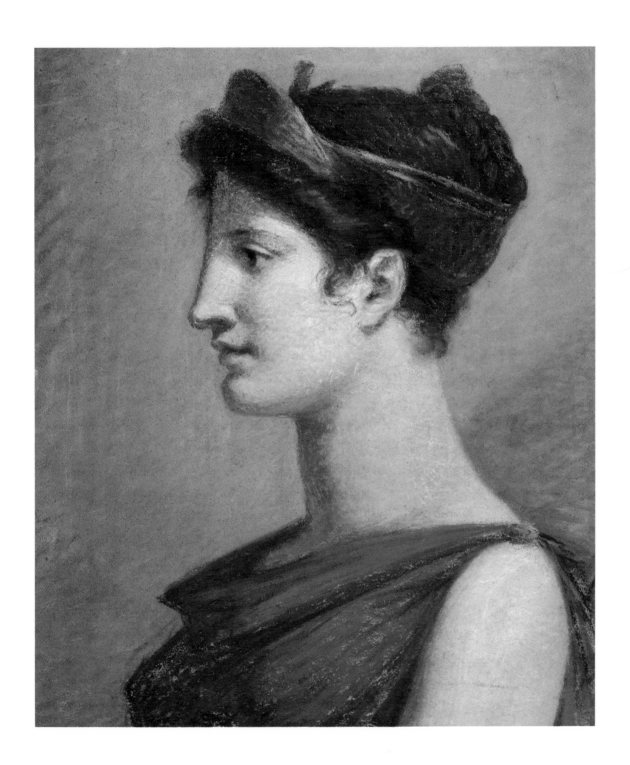

Pierre-Paul Prud'hon
(1758-1823)

Bust of a Young Woman
Wearing a Diadem, c. 1804.
Pastel on canvas.

19th
century

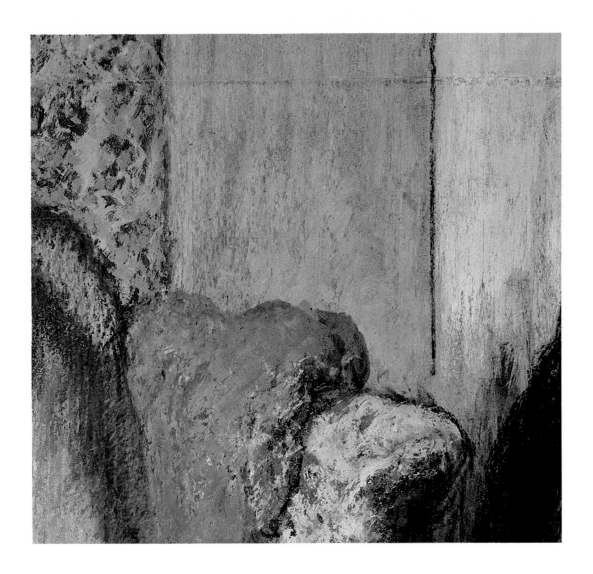

A century
of liberation and invention

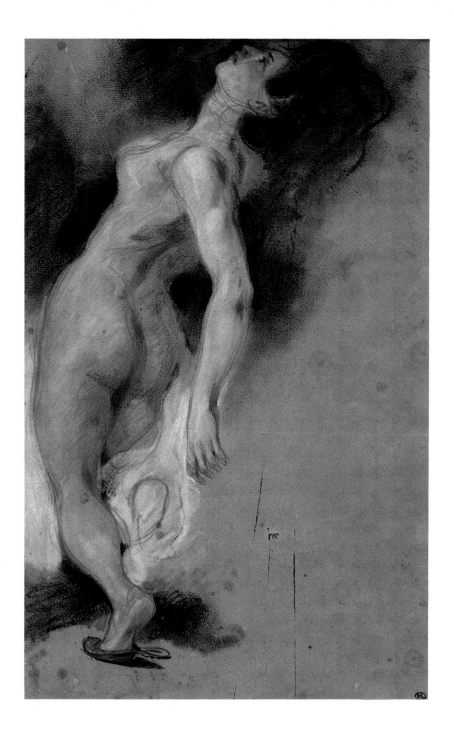

Eugène Delacroix
(1798-1863)
Sketch for The Death
of Sardanapalus, c. 1827.
Pastel.

Edouard Manet
(1832-1883)
Méry Laurent with a Large Hat, 1882.
Pastel on cardboard.

Delacroix saw pastel as a highly suitable medium for preliminary studies for his large paintings; it was flexible, quick, allowed him to indicate colours and highlights, and gave him a rough sketch of form, outline and lighting. This pastel sketch of a nude woman for his early painting *The Death of Sardanapalus*, showing her bent over backwards and about to be stabbed (her assailant is not visible here), captures movement, volume and light effects all in one. Delacroix used pastel not only for figures but also for landscape studies, chiefly twilight and night scenes, in an early nineteenth-century anticipation of subjects that the Impressionists were to take further.

For Manet, working almost half a century later, pastel was not just a way of studying an oil painting before tackling the final version but a self-sufficing medium that enabled him to produce highly finished portraits, whether bust or half-length, in profile or three-quarter view. As regards technique, while he very often used a canvas support for his pastels, Manet was also fond of cardboard, which must have suited him with its matt finish and which he occasionally allowed to show through in places. The density of his pastel comes from his rubbing large flat areas with a stump; he used few colours, with black usually paramount —that peculiarly intense black that we find throughout his work— as in this portrait of *Méry Laurent with a Large Hat*, which features one of the painter's favourite models. The relief on the face is very light, stressing principally the eyes, nostrils and lips. The impression given is one of great expressive mobility, and the delicacy of this is in marked contrast to the dark mass of the suit and hat. Manet hardly ever specified his backgrounds, giving them one colour only—though there is movement here too— with a strong predilection for greys and pinkish beiges.

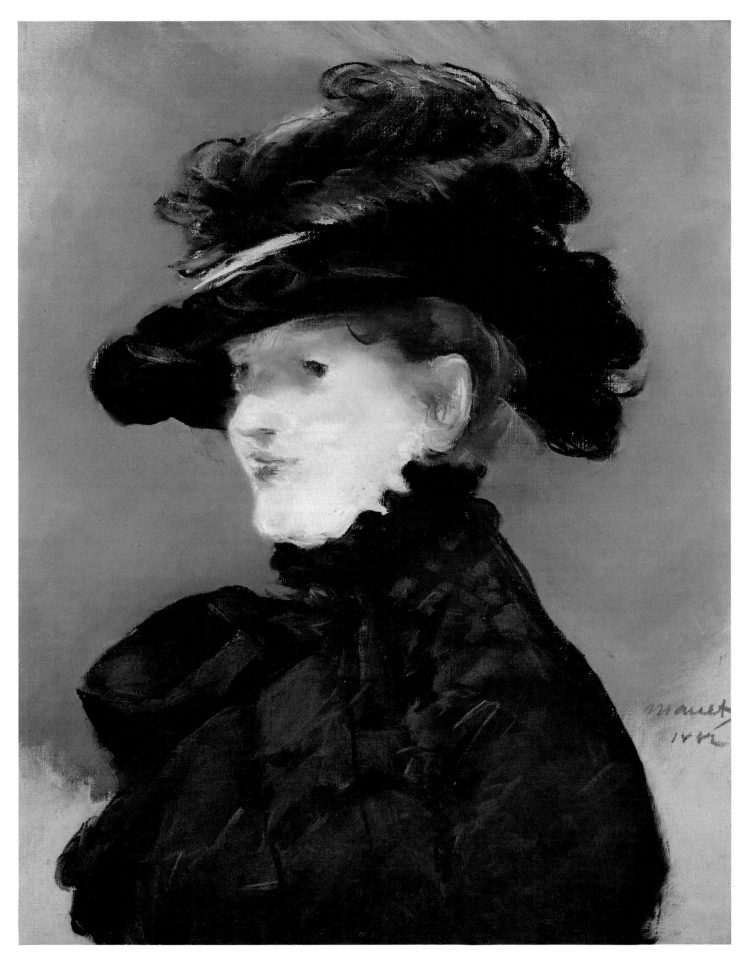

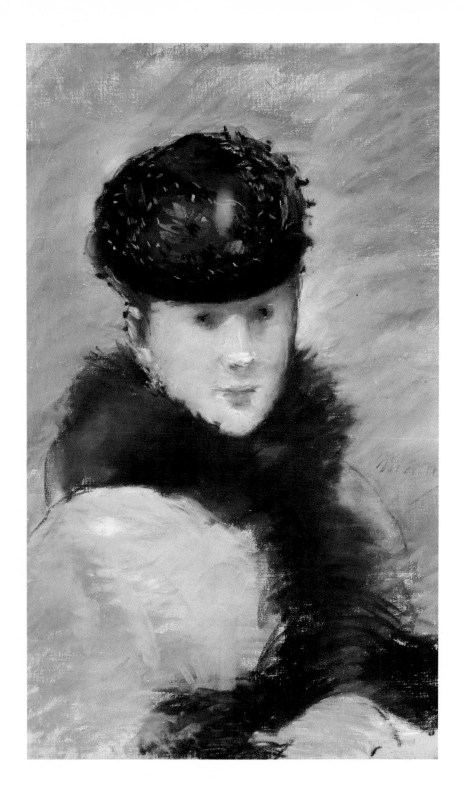

Edouard Manet
(1832-1883)
Méry Laurent with a Small Toque, 1882.
Pastel on canvas.

Edgar Degas
(1834-1917)
Star Dancer on Stage, c. 1878.
Pastel.

The nature of pastel powder is such that it offers two very different possibilities: sharp contours defined by lines or hatching may be overlaid with one or more coats of powder concealing the drawing and obscuring the shapes. By applying the finishing touches with a stump, Manet achieved a perfect harmony from this duality, this contrast.

Degas occasionally combined in one picture certain very precise elements such as an attitude or a face with other elements that he left unclear in shaded areas. *The Star Dancer on Stage* is an example of this, showing several important Degas inventions: the impression of artificial light illuminating the body of the dancer from below, picking out her throat and chin with a flash of white, the diagonal composition (a large void in the lower left-hand portion of the picture corresponds to the stage), and the dazzling colours (red, green, turquoise, orange, yellow) laid down in brisk zigzags, the strokes being left clearly visible. Here pastel possibly conveys better than oils all the speed, indeed instantaneity, of the subject, which is what Degas was after.

The brightest colours co-exist side by side and even overlap, set off by contrasting browns or blacks, as in the silhouette of a man in evening dress standing out of sight behind the set, which is briefly sketched in with a few strokes.

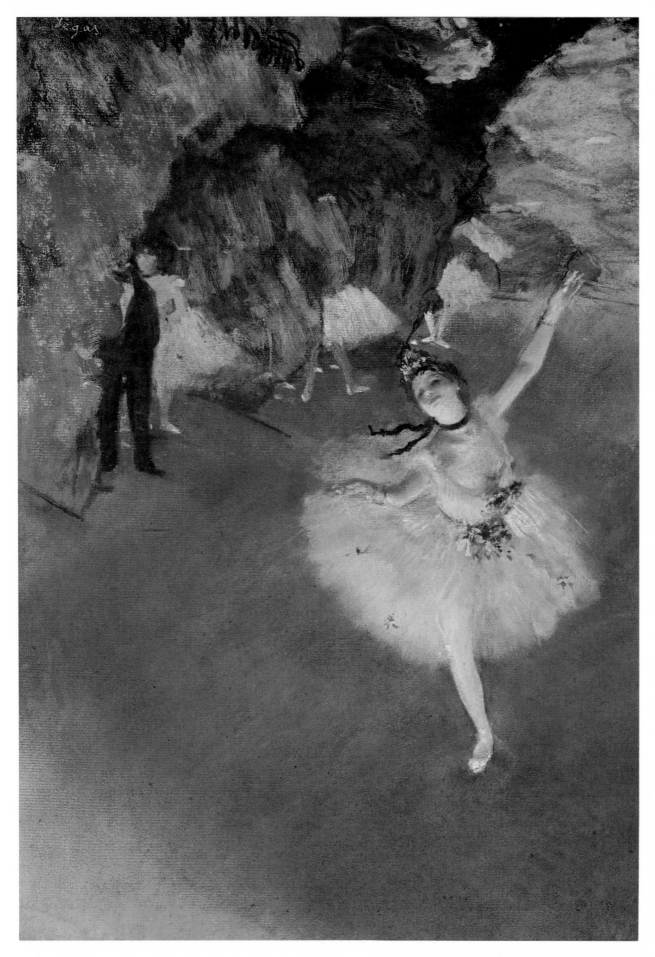

The new angles of focus used by Millet in the 1860s stem essentially from his choosing isolated figures and studying them in close-up, to borrow a term from the language of photography and the cinema. Millet's other, parallel invention was drawing with heavy hatching in pure colour. This twofold innovation, which arose out of the very nature of the pastel medium, was to

The unusual pose emphasized by hatching

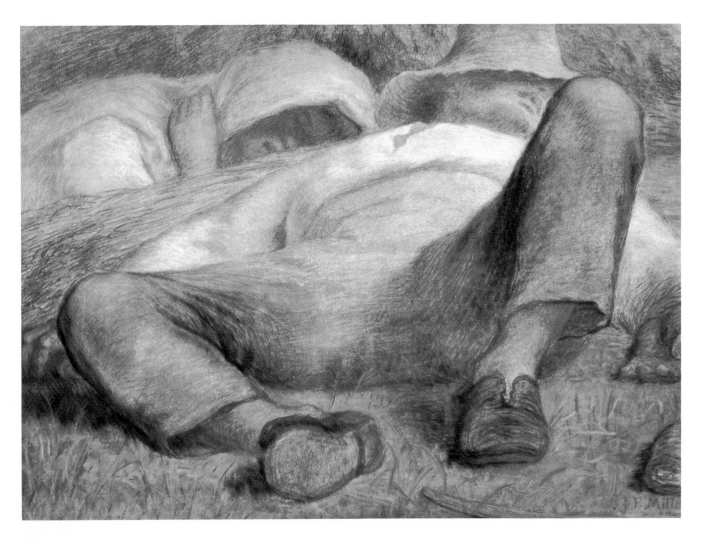

Jean-François Millet
(1814-1875)
The Noonday Rest, c. 1865.
Pastel.

Edgar Degas
(1834-1917)
Café Singer Wearing a Glove, 1878.
Pastel and tempera on canvas.

influence several later artists such as Degas, Van Gogh, and eventually Picasso. In *The Noonday Rest* the painter's eye is level with the ground on which the two figures are stretched out asleep. Millet came to his use of pure colour by progressive stages: from the 1850s he used pastel only for adding colour highlights to the black-crayon lines of his preliminary drawings; the black crayon gradually disappeared, leaving the pastel on its own.

Degas owned several of Millet's works (as the catalogue of the 1918 sale of Degas's collection shows), and their influence on him is obvious. He took the importance of focus and the use of faces seen in close-up a stage further. But he laid even greater emphasis on lighting that picked out the relief of features from

below (heavy white hatching bars his café singer's throat, chin, mouth, cheek-bones, and eyelids).

To a greater extent than Millet, Degas went in for strident colours and tonal relationships (e.g. gold, brown, salmon pink, green) set off by a few blacks (the glove worn by his café singer, Mademoiselle Desgranges, as we know the lady to have been, and the background on the right against which her head stands out). The strangeness of the composition is brought out by having the arm cut diagonally across the part of the background in which the colours unfold in vertical bands of different widths. Degas made a point of diversifying the texture of his paintwork, using moistened pastels for his flat tints, while he employed dry, powdery pastel to hatch certain details.

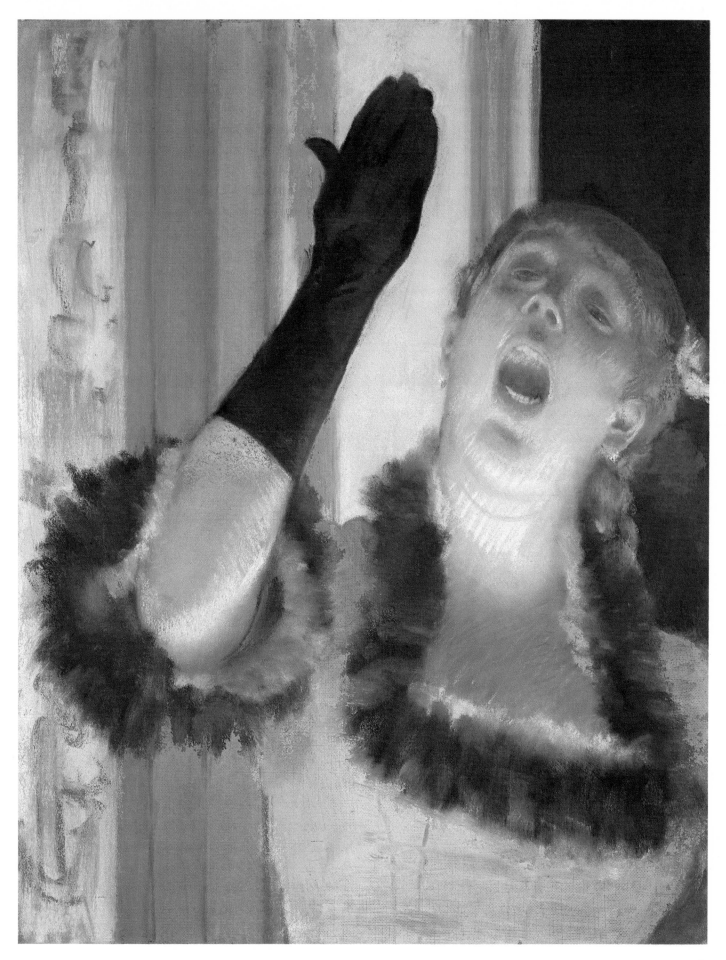

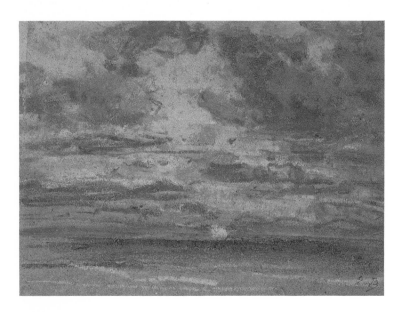

Eugène Boudin
(1824-1898)
Sky Study, c. 1859.
Pastel.
Detail page 54.

Eugène Boudin was one of the first, in the mid-1850s, to exploit the lightness of pastel in sky- and seascapes and beach scenes with people strolling about. Exhibited at the 1859 Salon, these studies attracted the admiring attention of Baudelaire, who wrote in his review: "If they [i.e. artists] had seen what I saw recently at Monsieur Boudin's... several hundred pastel studies improvised in front of the sea and sky, they would understand something they do not appear to have realized, namely the difference between a study and a painting... These amazing studies, so swiftly and so faithfully jotted down from subjects that could not be more inconstant, more elusive in terms of form and colour, in other words from waves and clouds, bear in the margin of each one the date, the time of day, and the wind; one, for example, reads: *8 October, noon, wind from the north-west.* If you have ever had the leisure to become acquainted with these meteorological beauties, you could verify from memory the accuracy of Monsieur Boudin's observations. With one hand covering the caption, you could guess the season, the time of day, and the wind. I am not exaggerating. In the end all those clouds with their fantastic, luminous shapes, those confused shadows, those green and pink immensities hanging in the sky piled one on top of the other,... all those depths and splendours, all this went straight to my head like strong drink or opium. And curiously enough, not once did it occur to me, gazing at those liquid or aerial spells, to complain about the absence of man."

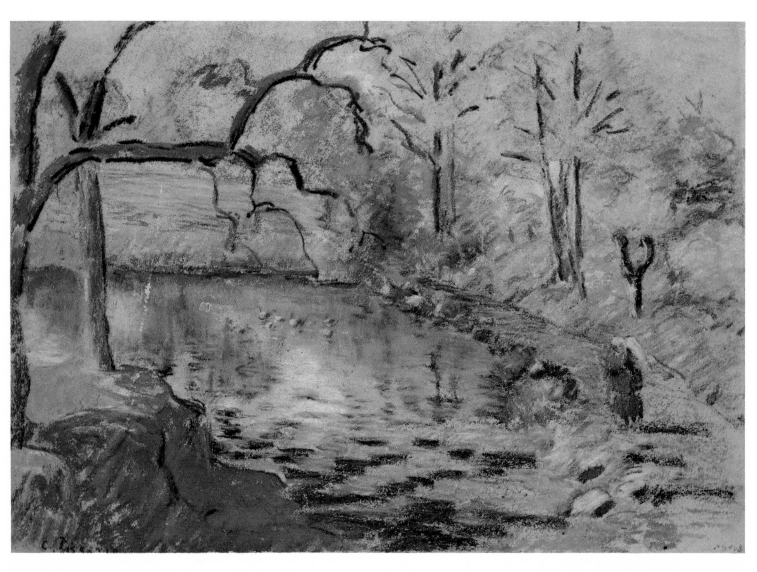

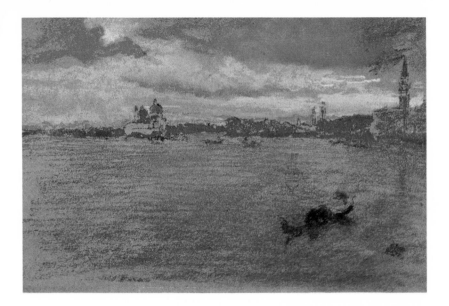

James McNeill Whistler
(1834-1903)
Stormy Sunset, Venice, 1880.
Pastel on brown paper.
Detail page 55.

Camille Pissarro
(1830-1903)
The Pond at Montfoucault, Autumn,
c. 1874-1875.
Pastel.

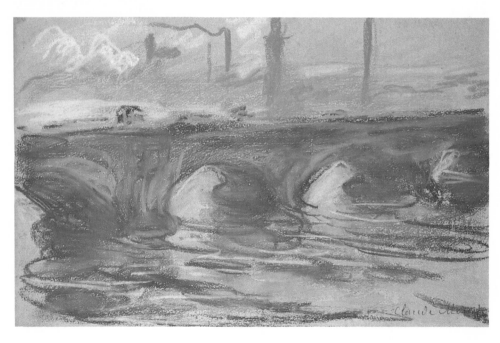

Claude Monet
(1840-1926)
Waterloo Bridge, London,
1900-1903.
Pastel.

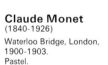

Twenty years before Monet and his painting *Impression, Sunrise*, Boudin anticipated that fresh way of transcribing light effects and the artist's response to them which the Impressionists were to evolve during the 1870s and after. In small-size studies consisting of a few strokes of grey, blue, pink, and gold, he recorded in pastel his vision of space in this *Sky Study*.

What Pissarro recorded in *The Pond at Montfoucault* (also called *The Watering Place*) was a mood and moment of autumn. Another version of this picture, also in pastel, shows the same landscape in summer. Pissarro began using pastel during the 1870s, starting with a number of finished drawings which he heightened and reworked. Here he was concerned to obtain different textures: flat and shaded for the surface of the water, uneven and striated for the trees and background.

Whistler, already known for his Symbolist-inspired compositions with their Oriental echoes, received a commission in 1879 to produce twelve etchings of Venice in three months. In fact he stayed for almost fourteen months in the city, and in addition to the etchings he brought back a whole series of pastels, fifty-three of which were exhibited at the Fine Arts Society in London in 1880. Venice fascinated him, of course. In his *Nocturnes* he had already delighted in capturing the fluidity of the Thames, and he had spent a great deal of time in the London museums studying Canaletto's *vedute* as well as Chinese landscapes with their extraordinary elliptical notation. His pastels seize all the magic of Venice, but they do so with a quite *un*melancholy joy; *Stormy Sunset*, saturated in blue and yellow, is alive with variations of light and reflections, the silhouettes of houses and palaces hinted at in the distance against a background of storm clouds and a sky streaked with pink.

Monet, in a fairly late pastel, *Waterloo Bridge, London*, used the medium to create an impression of something seen indistinctly through the fog. By concentrating on the reflections of the sky in the water he managed to convey the indissociable aspect of the two elements, the clouds and the river coming together within the same subdued range of greys, mauves, and blues.

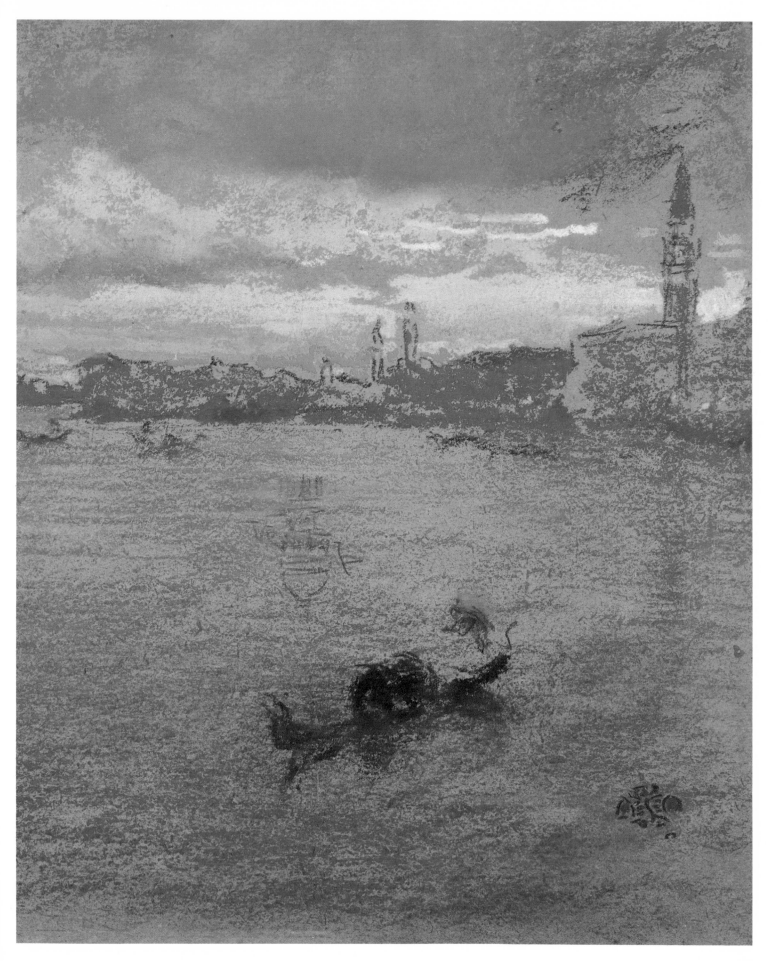

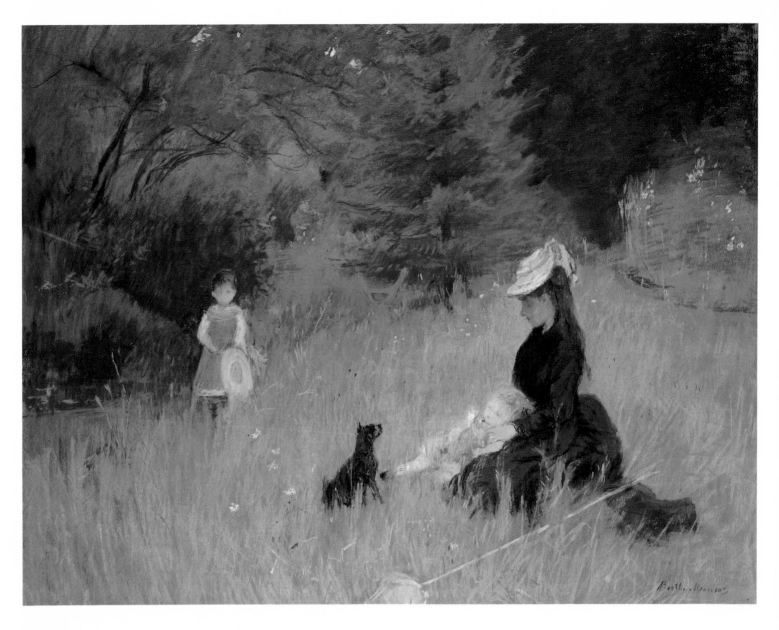

Berthe Morisot
(1841-1895)
In the Grass (The Artist's Sister
Edma Pontillon and her Children), 1874.
Pastel.

The lights of Impressionism

The two women painters of Impressionism, Berthe Morisot and Mary Cassatt, have many points in common and both produced a large body of pastels. They used the medium for its luminous texture, well suited to rendering light effects in the open air. Both had a predilection for garden scenes, with a profusion of trees, lawns and flowers. Both recorded the fleeting moments of summer days, intimist scenes of daily life, like siestas, games or reading. Berthe Morisot preferred the active figures of playing children; Mary Cassatt kept almost exclusively to the theme of motherhood, with babies cradled in the arms of their mother or nurse, often studied from close at hand. Both liked to use pastel in thick textures, traversed by broad hatchings, in harmonies of green, blue, white and pink rhythmed with accents of black. After participating in several of the impressionist exhibitions, they joined in 1877 the group of Independents, together with

Monet, Degas, Pissarro and Sisley, who refused to accept the notion of a jury empowered to judge the work of other artists and distribute medals and awards at the Salon exhibitions.

In the Grass dates from 1874, the year of the first group exhibition of the Impressionists, held in Paris in the studios of the photographer Nadar. Berthe Morisot took part in this and subsequent impressionist exhibitions, except that of 1878, when her daughter Julie was born. Berthe Morisot's style answers perfectly to the impressionist aesthetic: bright colours, vivid lights, fluid and separate brushstrokes, with a palette close to that of Renoir. She succeeds admirably in catching gleams of light and integrating figures into the open-air landscape.

Mary Cassatt joined the group of Independents in 1877, when Degas invited her to, after seeing some of her work in her studio. They became friends, and Degas initiated Mary Cassatt into certain technical details in his own handling of pastel, such as the use of tempera, turpentine and sprays in combination with it. Both had an unbounded admiration for Japanese prints: together they visited the big exhibition of 1890 at the Ecole des Beaux-Arts in Paris, which brought together over a thousand prints, and where Mary Cassatt purchased a hundred of them.

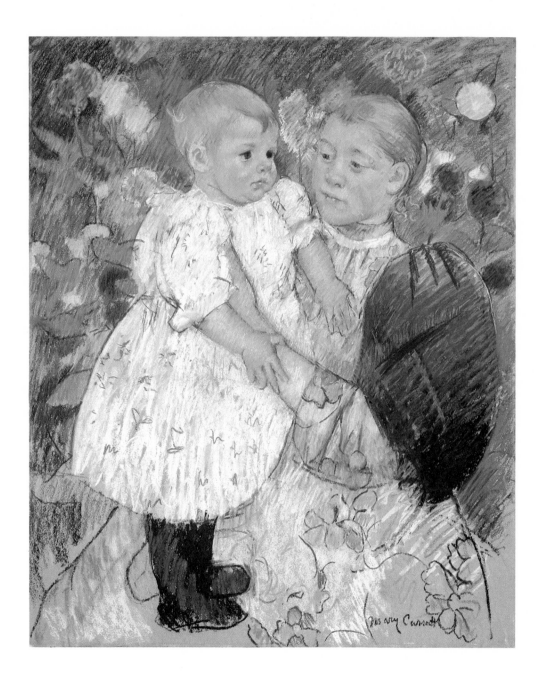

Mary Cassatt
(1845-1926)
In the Garden, 1893.
Pastel.

This pastel *In the Garden* may be dated to 1893, when Mary Cassatt had reached a turning point in her career, for that was the year of her one-man show at the Durand-Ruel Gallery in Paris, where she exhibited 108 works. The influence of Japanese art can be seen in the simplification of the motif, the well-knit design, the presence of a diagonal line dividing the figure group in two, and the decorative use of flower patterns on the fabrics alternating with the natural leafage in the background.

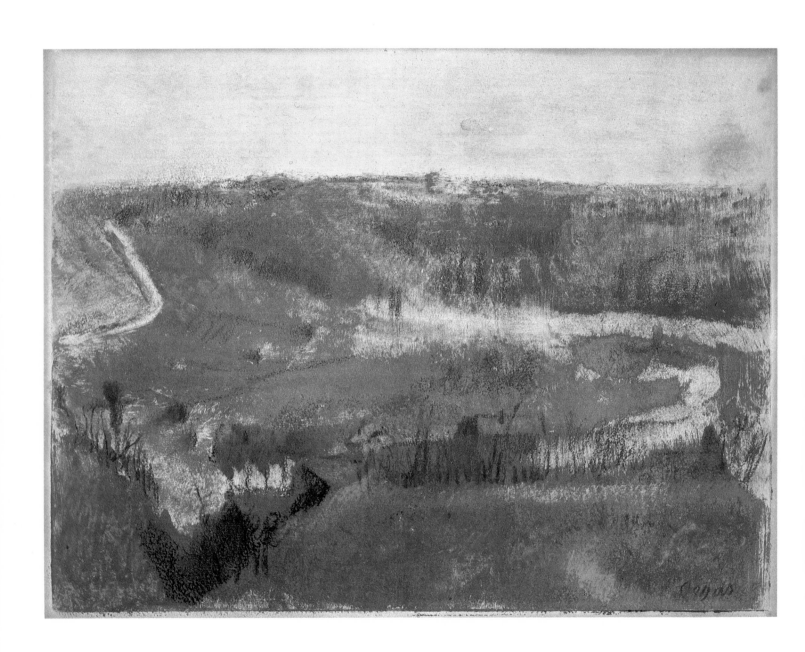

In his search for fresh textures and new effects Degas evolved the technique known as monotype. He applied oil-based ink or oil paint to a zinc or copper plate; he then subjected the ink or paint on the plate to various processes of obliteration, rubbing, or scraping before covering it with a sheet of damp paper and running the whole thing through the press. Usually he did not confine himself to a single print but kept on using the same plate until every scrap of paint had been absorbed. These residual impressions then provided the basis for fresh compositions that he worked over and heightened with pastel. In this way he executed a series of landscapes with a soft, blurred texture all their own, incorporating irregularities that stemmed from the marks of the brush, rag, pad, or fingers with which he had applied the ink or paint.

Degas was fascinated by the contrasts between the impression from the plate in the form of a reversed print and the pastel heightening that he applied to it directly, in other words by the interplay of textural effects between indirect application (by way of the plate) and drawing on the sheet of paper. Sometimes Degas generously moistened the pastel heightening in such a way as to obtain flat tints and streakings. Each colour was applied to the plate in a different manner—with a fine brush, with a

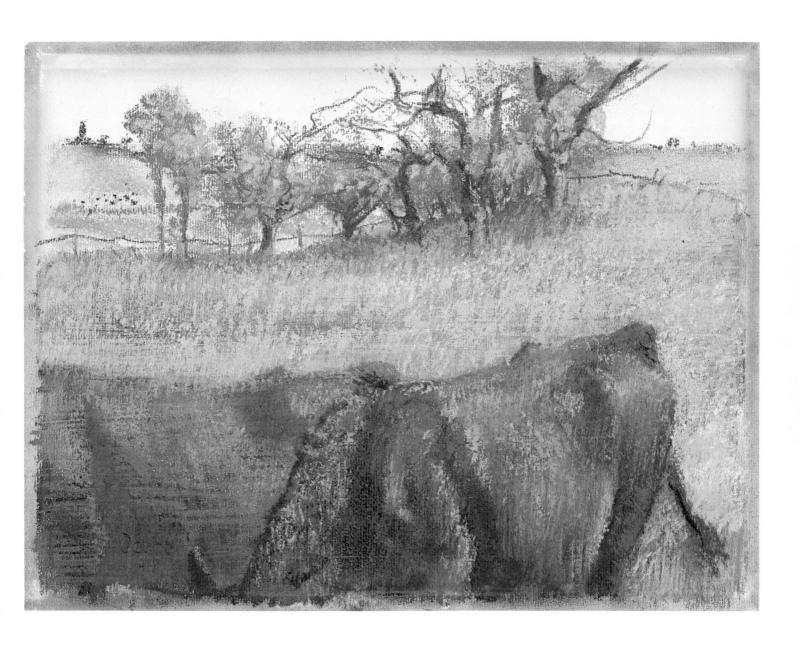

Edgar Degas
(1834-1917)

Landscape, 1890.
Monotype and pastel.

Landscape: Cows in the Foreground,
c. 1880-1890.
Pastel.

dry brush, with the points of the brush to suggest tufts of vegetation, in vertical lines to convey a mass of trees, these textural effects serving to differentiate the elements of the landscape: trees, grassy bank, a river in its valley. The experiments Degas made, both in monotype and pure pastel, were all to do with tactile perception.

Unlike his treatment of other subjects, his landscape work of the 1880s was done in a subdued colour scale: green, mauve, brown, beige, deep violet. The unclear outlines make the picture difficult to read but leave our minds free to wander at liberty through the landscape depicted.

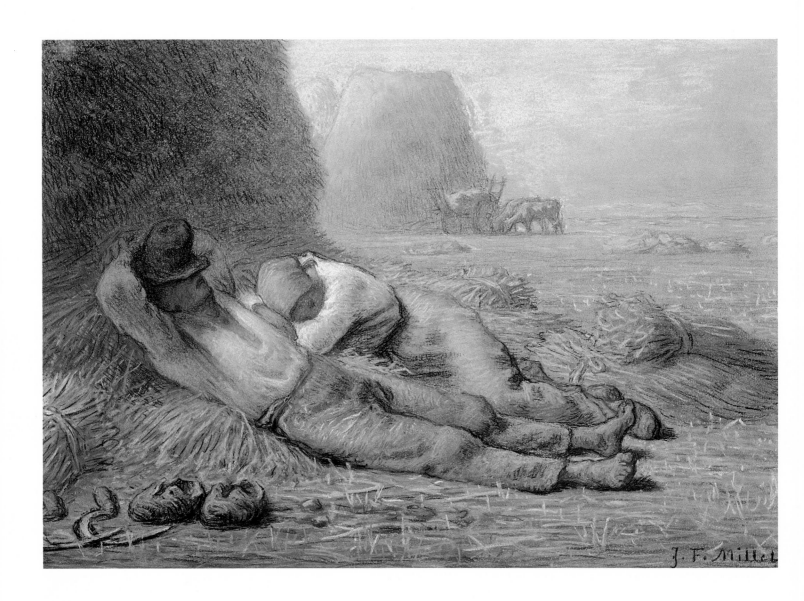

Jean-François Millet
(1814-1875)
The Noonday Rest, 1866.
Pastel and black crayon.

Henri de Toulouse-Lautrec
(1864-1901)
Portrait of Vincent van Gogh, 1887.
Pastel on cardboard.

Millet's *Noonday Rest* of 1866 gives us an instance of a texture blending pastel and black crayon. The contours and modelling are solidly structured with lines laid in with an unerring sureness of hand. This forcible drawing as well as the idea of hatching was later taken up by Van Gogh in other media. Some of Millet's finest pastels antedate the innovations of the Impressionists, and his influence marked their work in the pastel medium.

When Toulouse-Lautrec made his portrait of Vincent van Gogh (whom he had probably met in the studio of the painter Cormon towards the end of 1886), he was not unnaturally influenced by the technique of the artist to whom he was paying tribute. The hatchings flicker and whirl like an intricate maze of lines and interlacings forming a concentric web. The light, indicated by a few strokes of pastel colour, converges on the head seen in profile at the centre of the composition, facing right.

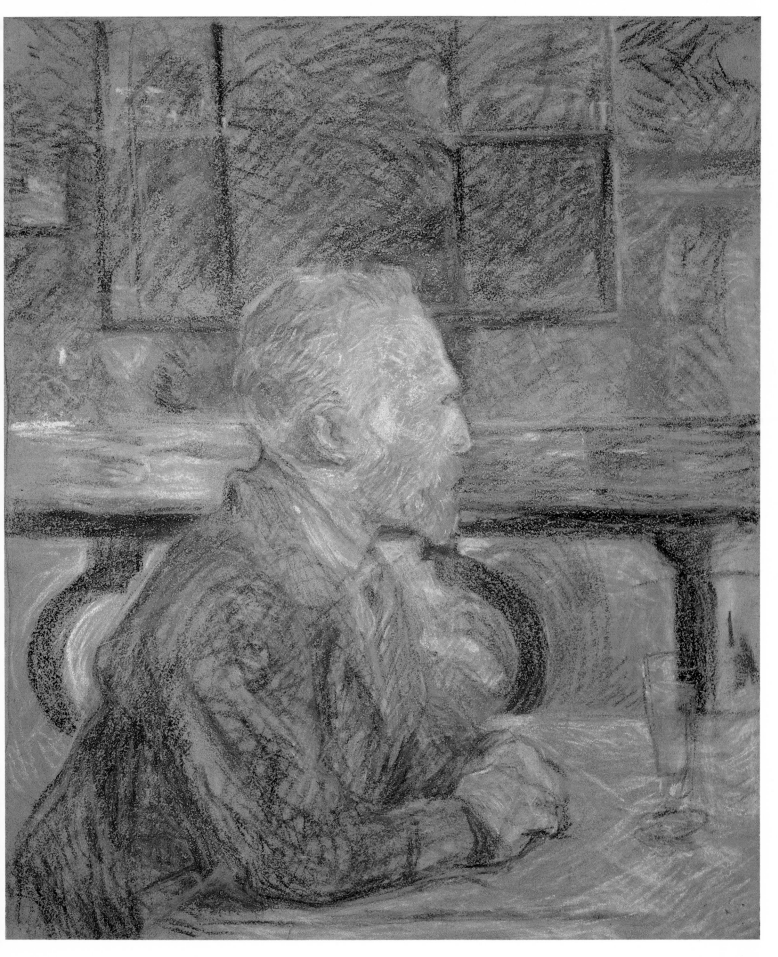

"We must stop painting interiors with people reading or women knitting. We must create living characters who breathe, feel, suffer and love. I shall do a series in this vein. The public will grasp the sacred nature of the subject and take off their hats as they do in church," Munch wrote in his *Diary* in 1889. And in Berlin in the final months of 1893, having deliberately cut himself off from all his friends, he embarked upon the great cycle of paintings that

Sharply outlined forms

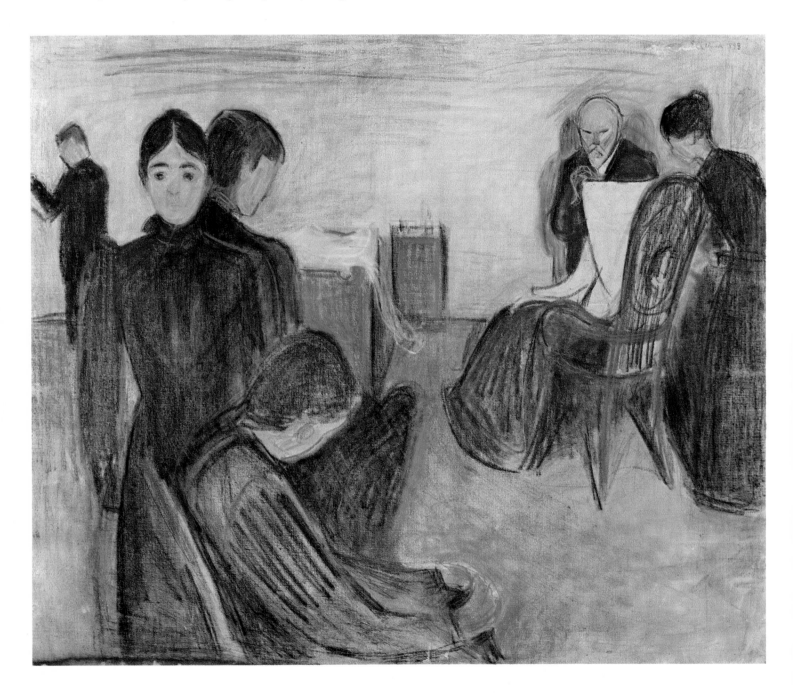

Edvard Munch
(1863-1944)
Death in the Sickroom, 1893.
Pastel.

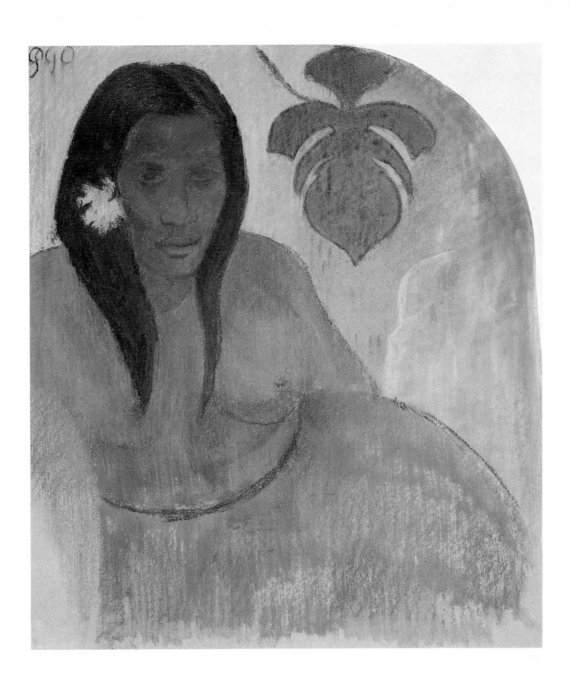

Paul Gauguin
(1848-1903)
Woman of Tahiti, c. 1891.
Pastel.

he intended should be exhibited together in the manner of a frieze, the magnificent *Frieze of Life*.

Of the seven paintings of this cycle completed between August and November 1893, *Death in the Sickroom* is the most monumental. One version of it was executed in pastel, which "gave the painting the character of a fresco" (Otto Benesch). Munch applied his pastel in broad parallel streaks that follow the movements and attitudes of his figures, giving them great dramatic emphasis. The linework is tailored to the dynamics of each figure, enabling it to synthesize three key functions: gesture, colour, and simplification. Munch often omitted certain details of the facial features in order to bring out a particular element —the eyes, for instance— which then constitutes the focus of the composition.

In the case of Gauguin the thickness of the line left by the pastel stick chimed with the need he often felt to enclose his figures in thick outlines. He also occasionally turned to pastel for its light, hazy quality, using it in conjunction with gouache. This blend of powdery pastel with the opacity of gouache gave Gauguin an

unusual medium capable of producing some uncommon colour nuances that were just what he needed to modulate the strange and exotic figures, half real, half imaginary, that people his Tahitian scenes and landscapes.

There are noticeable stylistic similarities between Munch and Gauguin in terms of this use of the monumental on an almost mural scale. Both were adept at having a frontal figure occupy the foreground with an insistent gaze that catches and holds our attention. Both men schematized, stylized, and synthesized faces and the thick outlines enclosing forms. They imparted a sense of rhythm to curves of expressive amplitude. They had the same feeling for abstract colours that corresponded neither to nature nor to reality but to their own inner vision, which brought them close to the Symbolist approach and even closer to that of the Expressionists. There is no proof that the two artists ever met. However, Gauguin did exhibit alongside Norwegian artists at Kristiania (Oslo) in 1885, and Munch may have encountered his work at that time, in other words before his own trip to France in the following year, 1886, and his subsequent visits to Paris.

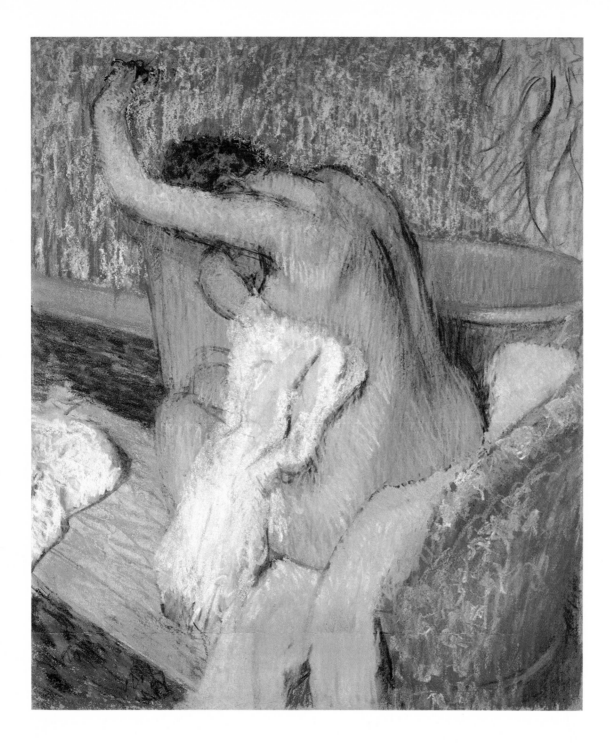

Edgar Degas
(1834-1917)

After the Bath: Woman Drying Herself, 1889-1890. Pastel and watercolour on board.

Auguste Renoir
(1841-1919)

Two Young Women or Conversation, 1895. Pastel.

In the pastels that he did in the 1890s Degas used the medium in a new way. Over sixty now and with failing eyesight, he nevertheless managed to give his surface textures a power that possibly no one before him had attained in pastel, using a less precise linear design, retracing his contours with numerous alterations, and superimposing layers of different colours. He also made a point of varying the execution, using parallel lines or criss-cross hatchings, zigzags, short broken strokes, and white chalk highlights. The overlaying of each coat of colour, with their successive and unexpected tonal relationships, gave rise to some unusual harmonies. Form and colour merge in these pastels while the figure is more fully integrated into the background, the purely descriptive elements of which are as it were drenched in colour and light, anticipating the style of Vuillard and Bonnard.

Renoir's *Conversation*, a pastel of monumental conception, dates from 1895, in other words a time when the Impressionist experiment already lay in the past, and in it Renoir strove for maximum saturation with light in each shade of colour, blending in unruffled harmony the precision of his drawing, the sweep of his composition, the definition of the two attitudes, and the expression of instantaneity. The treatment in criss-crossing stripes creates an envelope of luminous highlights. Some of the broadly shaded or flattened hatching is echoed in finer lines on the surface. The finished execution and the very fact that the central figure group and the background are treated with equal prominence again suggest the parallel between pastel and oil painting. This pastel may possibly be an earlier variant of the painting on the same subject.

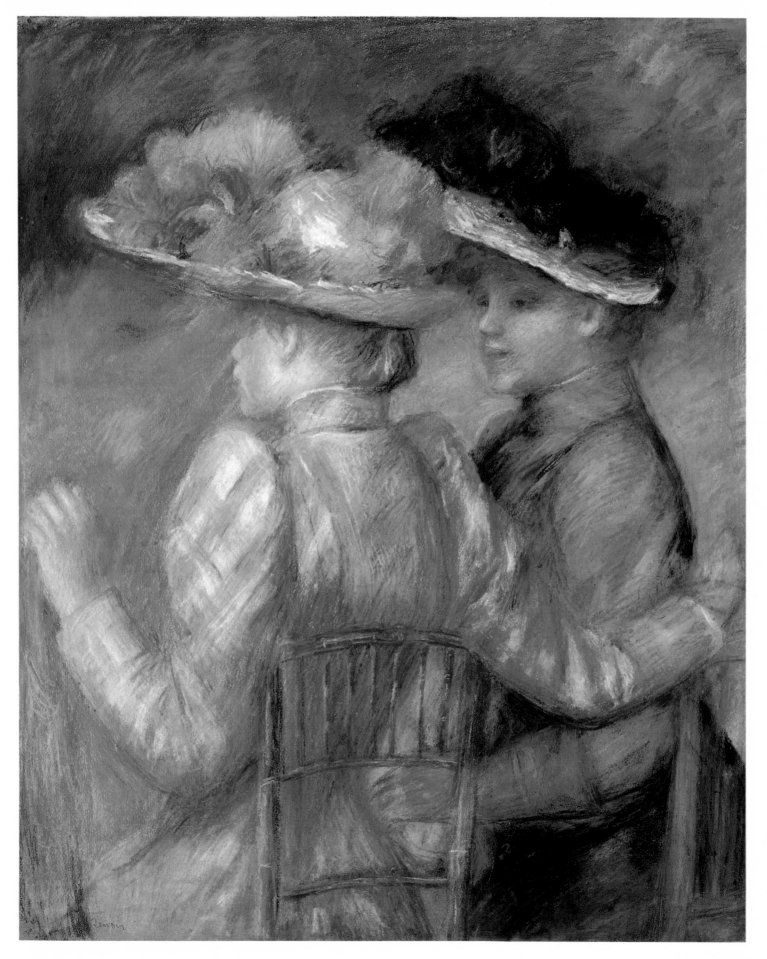

Toulouse-Lautrec saw pastel as a way of achieving extremes of colour when working on sketches for his oil paintings. The acidity of some of the hues in this pastel (absinthe green, salmon pink, violet pink, violet blue) was not reproduced in the final oil painting, which uses more subdued, almost faded tones, though retaining all the other elements of the composition as well as the attitudes of the figures. The pastel is treated in flat, uniformly

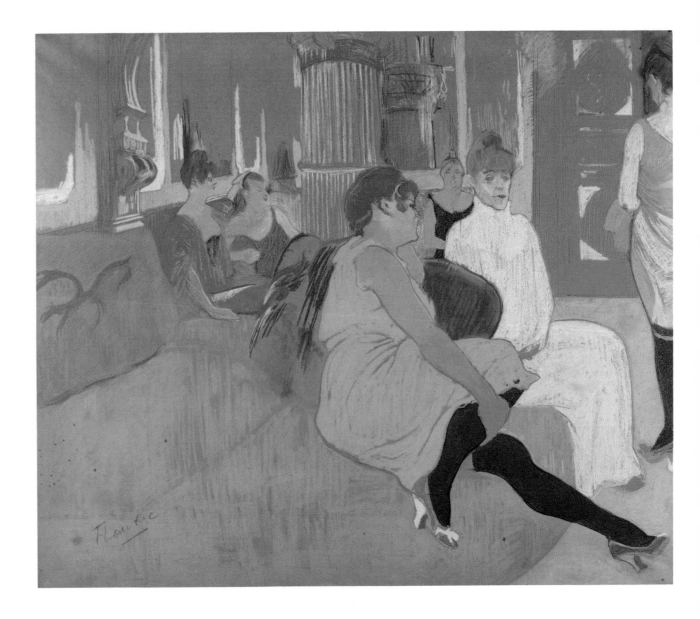

shaded areas that the artist has then gone over again with quick, flexible strokes which recall Lautrec's masterly knack of constructing a figure in a few lines, with the result that he often treated oil paint as if it had been pastel. This example, which dates from 1894, is executed entirely in the spirit of a brush and spirit-thinned oil-paint sketch, which was perhaps Lautrec's favourite technique.

In the autumn of 1901 Picasso left Barcelona for his second visit to Paris. There, in April 1902, he exhibited some paintings and pastels at the Berthe Weill Gallery. In Paris in 1901 he had painted his famous *Blue Room* or *La Toilette* (Phillips Collection, Washington), representing his studio in the Boulevard de Clichy: in this picture, pinned to the wall in the background,

Henri de Toulouse-Lautrec
(1864-1901)
The Drawing Room in the Rue des Moulins
(Women in a Brothel), 1894.
Pastel.

*The immediacy
of the snapshot*

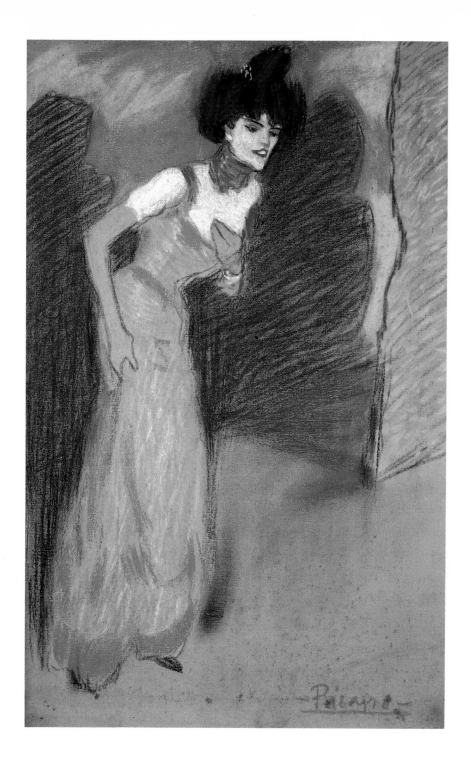

Pablo Picasso
(1881-1973)

Cabaret Singer Taking her Bow,
1900-1901.
Pastel on canvas.

figures Toulouse-Lautrec's May Milton poster, vouching for the young Picasso's continuing interest in this artist. Already in early drawings and pastels done in Madrid and Barcelona, he had taken over characteristic themes of Lautrec and also of Steinlen; he admired their easy knack of conjuring up a figure and fixing its pose with the immediacy of a snapshot. Like Degas and Lautrec, who delighted in such subjects, Picasso in this pastel focused his sharp eye on a cabaret singer lit up by the footlights. With spontaneous crayon strokes he schematizes the angular face and stooping figure, as she bows to the public at the end of her turn. The pastel medium enables him to modulate his vigorous contrasts to best effect. The handling is terse, spirited, rapid, with sharp outlines incising the silhouette.

Redon's use of charcoal crushed over broad areas of high density —he called them his *"noirs,"* his blacks— led him naturally to an appreciation of the powdery quality of pastel, with which he was able to obtain similar compact layers. In the famous drawing entitled *Armour*, for which Redon used a combination of charcoal and Conté crayon, the suit protects and conceals from view a mysterious figure who is clearly silhouetted but only part of whose face is actually visible: one eye, the temple, and the bridge of the nose. The head of the figure is covered and as it were bristles with warlike spikes or symbolic spines. The single, Cyclopean eye was a source of great fascination for Redon, who printed several series of lithographs using this subject: a series dedicated to Edgar Allan Poe in 1882, one entitled *Origins* in 1883, *Night* in 1886, and *Dreams* in 1891; finally the three *Temptation of St Anthony* series published between 1888 and 1896 also featured the eye motif.

Pastel marked Redon's rediscovery of colour around 1895, and he made it one of his favourite techniques. He had begun with portraits from life such as that of *Madame Redon at her Embroidery* (1880), the simple profile presentation of which prefigured the kind of meditative approach that Redon was later to go into more deeply. These later works became increasingly creations in which imagination outweighs reality. Several of his themes (e.g. *Stained-Glass Window, Praying Women, Profile of Light, Virgin and Child, Angel, The Sacred Heart, The Red Thorns*) reveal the deeply mystical spirit that informed Redon's work.

The same kind of spiritual intensity is evident in *Blue Profile*, which shows an androgynous face with closed eyelids and lips pressed together as if in silent prayer. The angular features are sharply delineated with a stroke of pastel and stand out like a medallion profile against a gold ground worked in relief as if guilloched, calling to mind the gold backgrounds of medieval paintings. The blue is a product of superimposed crushings of pure pastel. The strangeness of this vision is heightened by the fragmentary way in which Redon framed the face, perhaps with a view to stressing the idea of a fleeting apparition.

Odilon Redon
(1840-1916)
Armour, 1891.
Charcoal and Conté crayon.
Blue Profile.
Pastel.

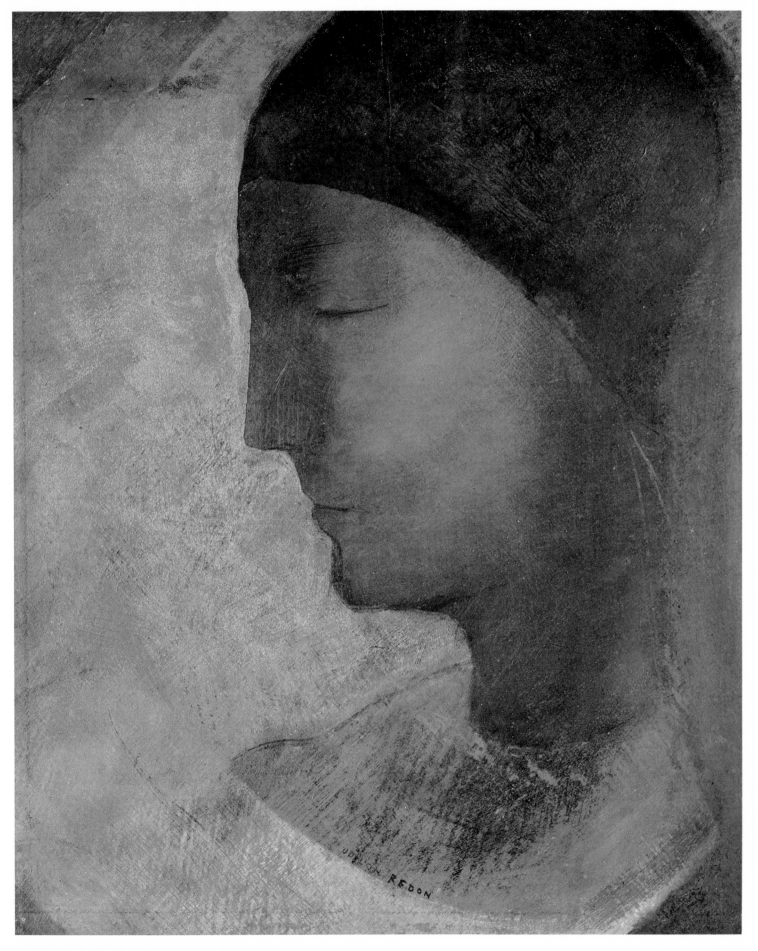

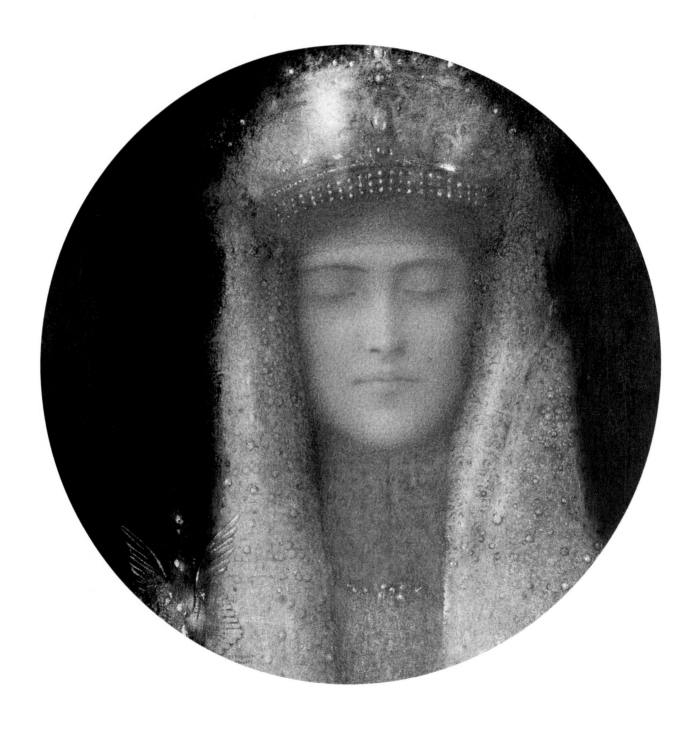

Fernand Khnopff
(1858-1921)
The Silver Tiara, c. 1900.
Pastel on cardboard.
The Sleeping Medusa, c. 1896.
Pastel.

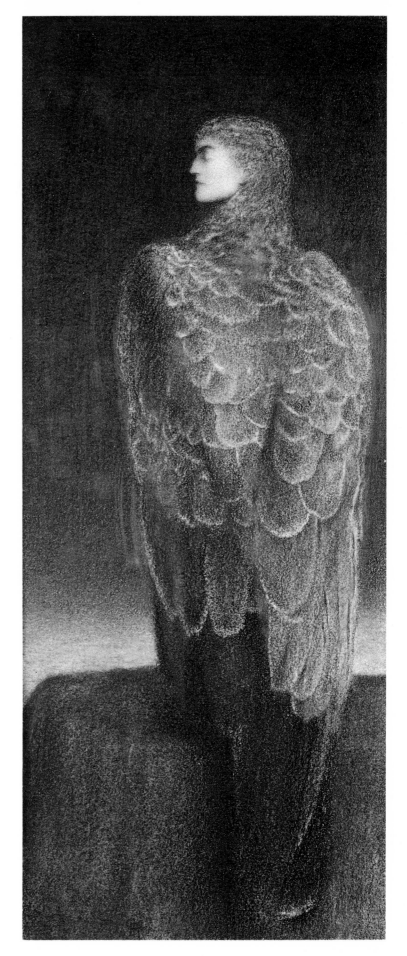

Khnopff was equally happy working with pastel and with coloured crayons, sometimes using both at once, one on top of the other. Coloured crayons offered a more precise, more delicate medium, the paler colours calling for a more meticulous treatment, while pastel offered greater intensity in terms of line, colour and grain. In fact one of the characteristics of Khnopff's work is this special grainy texture in the colouring medium, obtained without making use of the grain of the paper surface as Seurat did in his drawings. Khnopff's method was more like a dainty Pointillism, the pastel strokes just touching the paper very lightly.

In his study *The Sleeping Medusa*, signed and dating to about 1896, which shows her standing with wings folded and eyelids closed, Khnopff invented a strange figure —half eagle, half woman— to symbolize sleep, dreams, solitude, and the idea of remoteness. Khnopff's colour schemes often play on melancholy harmonies of white, grey and mauve. His faces are very pale, almost bloodless; they belong to creatures with reddish hair and strange-coloured eyes (like icy water or crystalline rock), wandering in another world than this, a world beyond the mirror. Their fixed and lifeless look is a key element here: either the eyes are staring intently or the eyelids are closed. The typically Symbolist theme of silence conveys the idea of the frontier between life and death. Even more mysterious, given the ambiguous nature of the figure's barely perceptible gaze, *The Silver Tiara* worn by a princess with a Madonna-like veil is executed in light touches of pastel blended into one another and shaded, creating a halo of iridescent light. She is the perfect epitome of all the hieratic female idols who sprang from the imagination of the Symbolists.

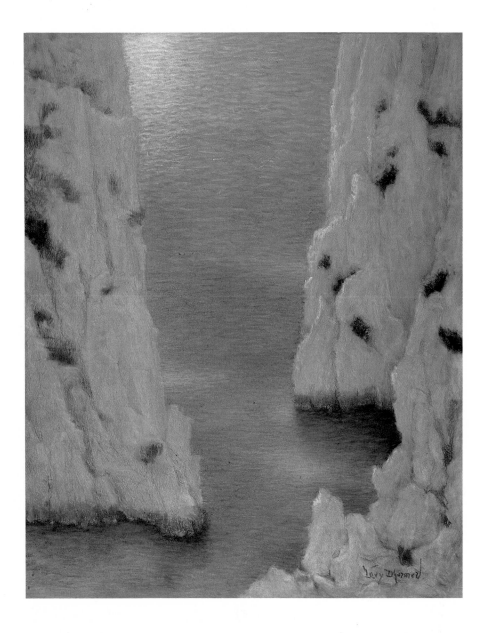

Lucien Lévy-Dhurmer
(1865-1953)
The Creek.
Pastel on paper.

**William Degouve
de Nuncques**
(1867-1935)
Peacocks, 1898.
Pastel on cardboard.

Segantini, though born in the same year as Khnopff and belonging like him to the Symbolist movement, nevertheless differed from him strongly in his very evident feeling for decoration. In this fan-shaped composition entitled *Love at the Well-Springs of Life* Segantini used a mixture of pastel and red chalk heightened with gold and silver on a vellum support. His style is closer to that of Art Nouveau, incorporating precious motifs and materials and influenced by Japanese art.

In the work of the Belgian artist Degouve de Nuncques these same Far Eastern influences were perfectly assimilated. Although in China peacocks are a symbol of wealth and prosperity, here they probably suggest the idea of the sun and of beauty and its intermittent transformations. The birds, depicted in light-hued colours, stand out amid a forest of dark pines, their luminosity in strong contrast to the casket of night that contains their spangled plumage. The pastel itself is in harmonies of green and blue applied in areas of flat, velvety colour. The decorative aim of the composition is emphasized by the play of lines, the verticals of the tree-trunks and the curves of the branches hanging down like the peacocks' wings.

Lévy-Dhurmer created some unusual landscapes with his choice of odd colour combinations —pinks and mauves, the epitome of Decadent stridency— though the shape and treatment of the rocks in *The Creek* correspond to a pretty accurate description of nature; the layout is odd, too, with its effect of squeezing this arm of the sea in the deep creek between the rocks.

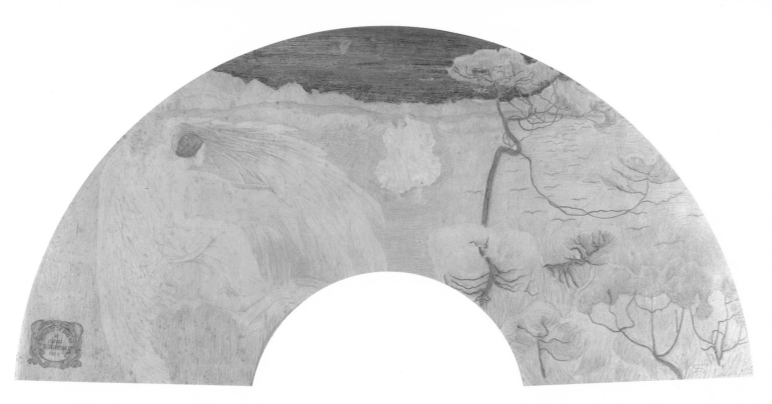

Giovanni Segantini
(1858-1899)

Love at the Well-Springs of Life, 1899.
Red chalk and pastel heightened with
gold and silver on vellum.

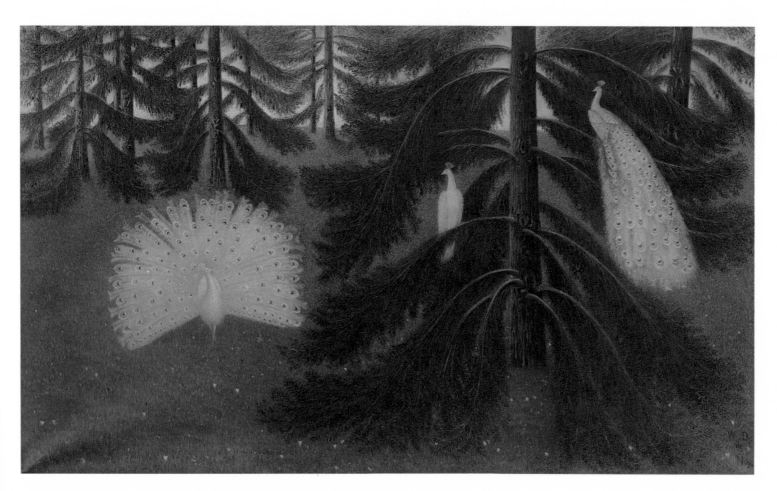

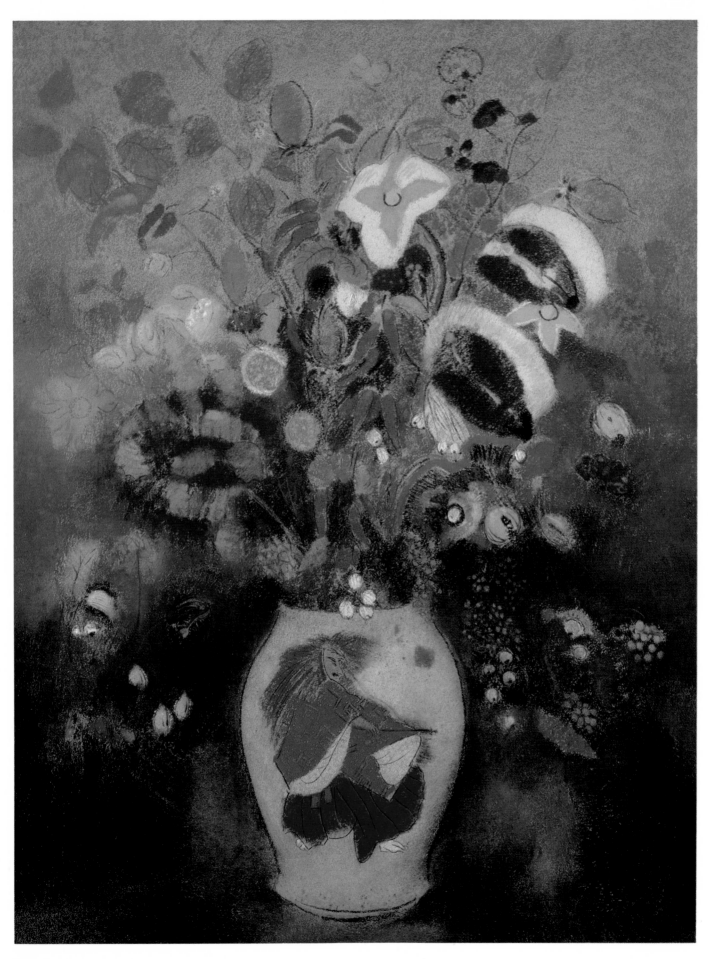

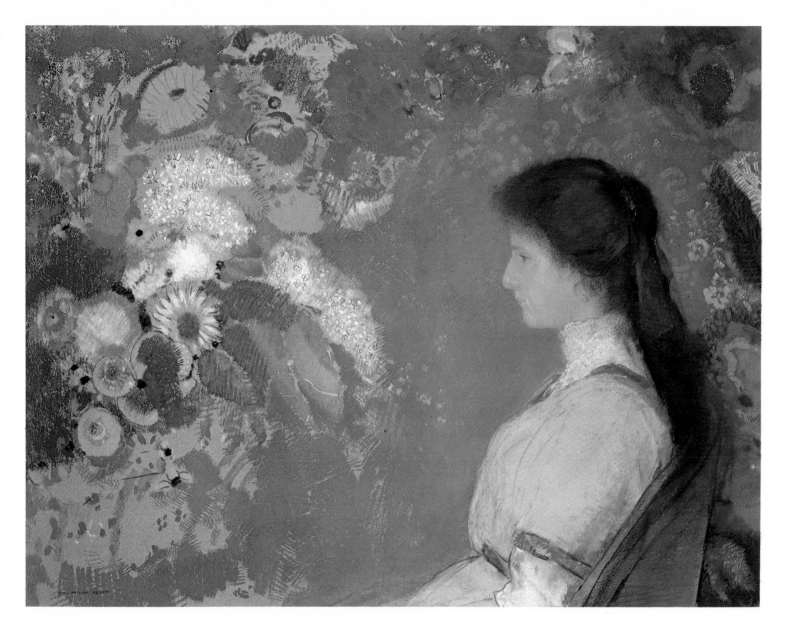

Odilon Redon
(1840-1916)
Flower Piece with Japanese Vase,
1905-1908.
Pastel.

Portrait of Mademoiselle
Violette Heymann, 1910.
Pastel.

"Breaths of colour"

In the early 1900s Redon began to devote a great many pastels to studies of bouquets of flowers, a subject he pursued in parallel with his underwater visions. Through these two subjects, in fact, the artist appears to have found release from anguish and symbolism of any kind and to have let himself go in order to create, with pastels of dazzling colours, compositions whose primary intention is decorative. Occasionally an ambiguous duality lingers on where a figure or a face emerges from amid an avalanche of flowers or a bed of seashells. While it is always possible in these works to recognize a real flower because of the attention we know Redon gave to every detail in his desire to "to work away in front of the object right down to the tiniest accidents of its visual appearance," as he wrote in his private diary (*A Soi-même*, Paris, 1922), nevertheless the chief impression conveyed is of the boundless wealth of his imagination. The Japanese

vase, on the other hand, is entirely real and belonged to the artist. The linear structure of Redon's earlier works, with the figures standing out against a background like that of a stained-glass window, has disappeared. From now on his work is all splashes of colour in broad flat tints or little touches floating all over the surface of the paper as if in suspension in what has become an abstract space.

Redon became progressively more responsive to the art of ceramics, silks, and tapestries. In 1910 he visited the Musée des Tissus or textile museum in Lyons, where he saw "marvels and relics whose beauty my eyes were doubtless prepared at that moment to drink in" (*Lettres d'Odilon Redon*, Paris, 1923). He used his pastels in pure colours laid side by side, giving rise to some unusual and intense harmonies of violet, carmine, blue and yellow.

75

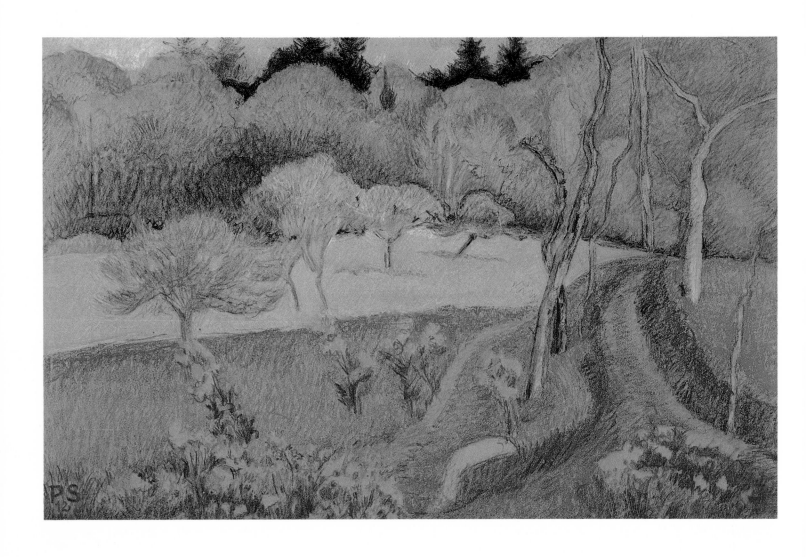

Paul Sérusier
(1864-1927)
Landscape, 1912.
Coloured crayons and
pastel on grey paper.

This Sérusier landscape of 1912, standing on the borderline bet-ween the real and the imaginary, was done on grey paper in a combination of coloured crayons and pastel. Space is suggested by a rhythmic pattern of decorative curves, creating distorted flat tints and modelling forms with unreal colours. The line of sight is placed fairly high. Individual crayon strokes and touches are unblended and distinct. This landscape of winding, ribbon-like lanes is one of a series of Breton landscapes painted by Sérusier and Gauguin in the years after they first met and worked together at Pont-Aven in the autumn of 1888. That same year, working under Gauguin's tutelage, Sérusier painted on the lid of a cigar-box the key picture known as *The Talisman* (or *Landscape in the Bois d'Amour*): it was this picture that in 1890 inspired Maurice Denis's famous definition of a modern painting as, before all else, ''a plane surface covered with colours assembled in a certain order.'' This set the orientation of the Nabis (from the Hebrew word meaning prophets), the group formed in 1892 which included Maurice Denis, Bonnard, Vuillard and Sérusier.

The transformation of perspective and the decorative treatment of this Breton landscape, with lanes as arabesques, go back to Gauguin but also have much in common with Matisse and the Fauves.

A favourite theme with Edouard Vuillard, one of the founders of the Nabi group, is the interior of his Paris studio, often with family or friends included in the scene. But he liked to look out from it too, painting what he saw. This pastel, of about 1915, is an off-centre view of the *Place Vintimille* as seen from his studio window. Paradoxically, it is carefully structured, even though conveying his impression of the square by broad hazy areas (the groups of trees, for example). This style is close to that of his oil paintings of this period. All in muffled contrasts and unexpected accords, heightened by lighting effects designed to unify figures and setting, this powdery, blurred, luminous style goes to create the habitual atmosphere of Vuillard's pastels.

Edouard Vuillard
(1868-1940)
View of the Place Vintimille
from the Artist's Studio, c. 1915.
Pastel.

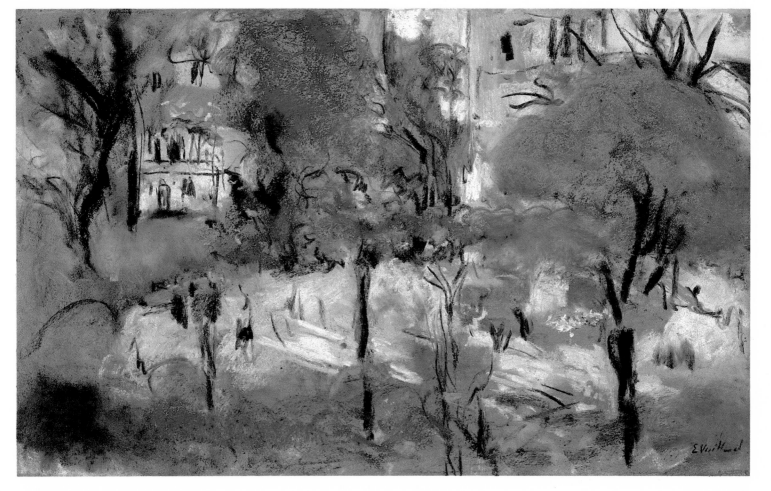

20th
century

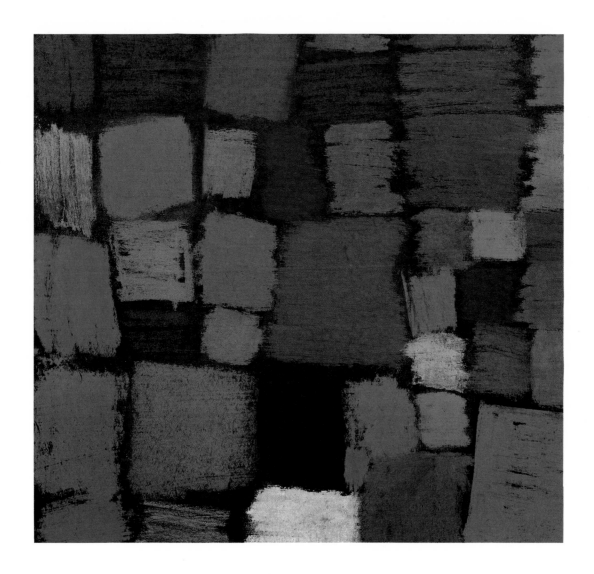

Pastel
as a creative challenge

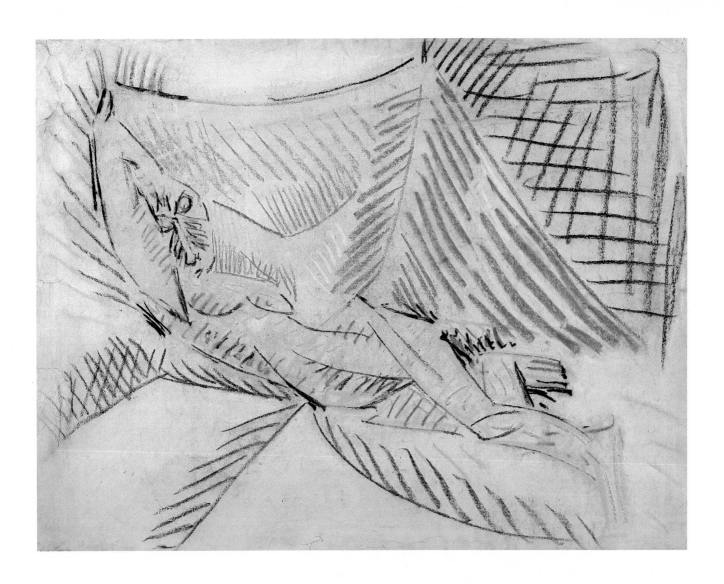

Line patterns

In the years 1901-1904 Picasso painted largely in a blue monochrome, producing an impressive series of figure compositions and self-portraits which break sharply with the Belle Epoque style of the previous years (see page 67). These pictures include pastels, treated in fine hatchings with stumped areas which go to create modelling. The summer of 1904 saw the beginning of his Rose Period, in which a similar monochrome was used with a new harmony and plenitude in the treatment of nude figures.

In the summer of 1907, following up the experiments which had culminated in the *Demoiselles d'Avignon* (1906-1907, Museum of Modern Art, New York), Picasso worked on his *Nude with a Drapery* (Hermitage, Leningrad). For this picture he made several pastel studies of details and figures closely related to those of the *Demoiselles d'Avignon*. These pastels mark a further stage in the simplification of forms, the distortion of bodies, the abstract geometrization of faces. He amplified the pattern of parallel hatchings of different colours occupying triangular, asymmetrical zones of space (closed eye, open eye) which prefigure the breakdown of volumes into multiple facets characteristic of Cubism in the years 1910-1911. The forms thus arrived at are imaginary forms treated in accordance with an abstract patterning and enclosed in narrow margins. This style of drawing stemmed from Picasso's discovery, in the summer of 1907, of African woodcarvings in the ethnographic rooms of the Trocadéro Museum in Paris.

Kirchner was fascinated by bursts of flamboyant colour and his sources of inspiration were similar to those of Fauvism. After an early period, in Dresden from 1905 on, of stylized forms and outright borrowings from the primitive arts, he went on towards a stricter design and a more controlled but ever more powerful affirmation of Expressionism.

All his work is distinguished by an unhesitating speed of execution. The very rapidity of the pastel strokes, applied in abrupt and jerky parallels, further emphasizes the deformation of the silhouettes and the distortion of the urban space —the streets of Berlin— in which they move. Here the central axis formed by the woman's long slender figure creates a dynamic composition with a pendulum system that animates the whole scene. This approach is similar to that of the Italian Futurists (Boccioni, Balla, Severini, Carrà). Like them, but independently, Kirchner conveys objects and settings from interacting viewpoints and, by way of that synthetic image, symbolizes movement and the idea of walking.

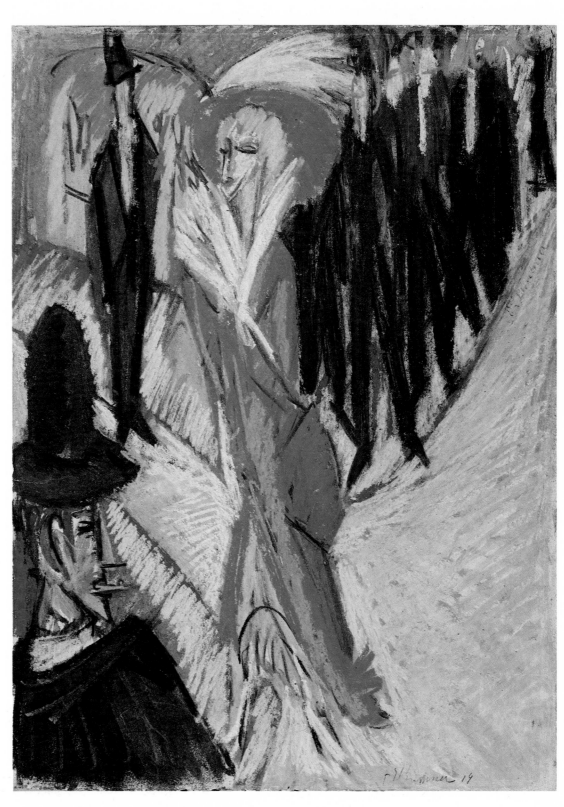

Pablo Picasso
(1881-1973)
Reclining Nude, summer 1907.
Pastel on paper.

Ernst Ludwig Kirchner
(1880-1938)
Street with Woman in Red, 1914.
Pastel over chalk on
yellow paper.

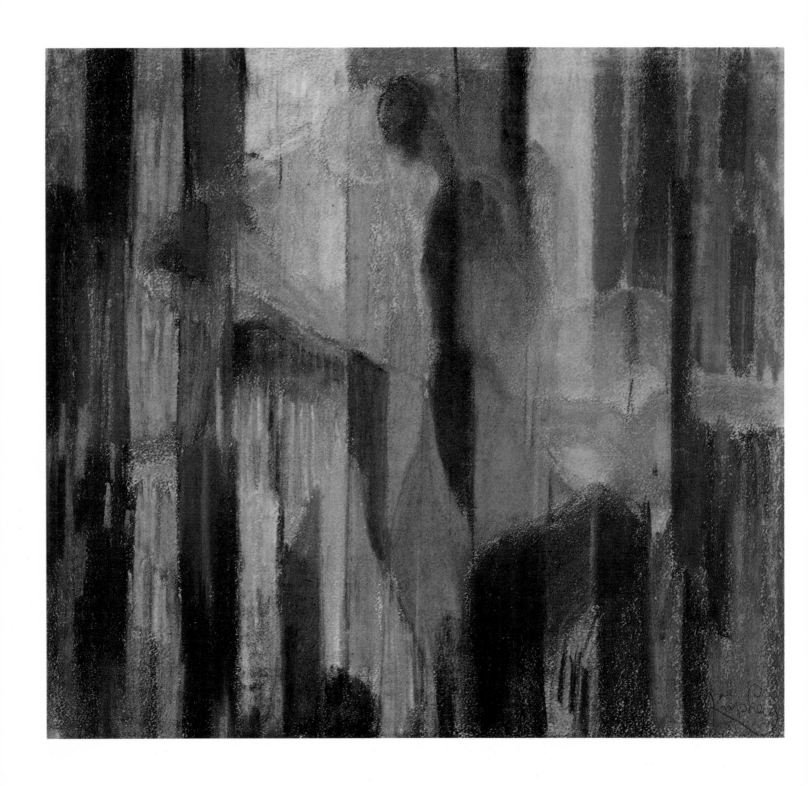

Frank Kupka
(1871-1957)
Woman Picking Flowers,
c. 1907-1908.
Pastel on white paper.

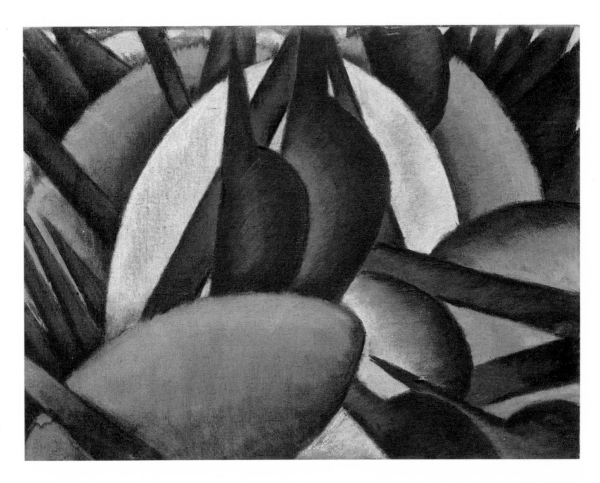

Arthur Dove
(1880-1946)
Plant Forms, 1915.
Pastel on canvas.

This pastel of a *Woman Picking Flowers* was painted by Kupka in 1907-1908, when the young Czech artist was combining abstract and figural elements, and expressing through colour their relation to movement and their breakdown into successive states across a given space. Broad vertical bands of pastel, in different colours, are cut off, divided into segments, by the interpenetration of the woman's silhouette in side view, as she walks and bends forward to pluck some flowers (she bends down obliquely, by degrees, towards the left side of the picture). Dividing the space into parallel sections, Kupka creates an interacting pattern, one vertical and fixed, like a grid through which the figure follows a double path of movement: the horizontal walking movement towards the left and the oblique trajectory of the stooping figure. Kupka made a series of at least fifteen studies of this theme, superimposing planes and colours in an interlocking pattern of geometric space. Here he used a wide range of colours: brown, orange, blue, violet, green and yellow; and he carried out a thorough pictorial analysis even while schematizing the figures.

With these experiments Kupka anticipated by several years the idea of a sequential breakdown of movement which Marcel Duchamp embodied in his famous, his notorious painting *Nude Descending a Staircase* (1912, Philadelphia Museum of Art). In Paris at that time, Kupka was friendly with Jacques Villon and his brothers Raymond Duchamp-Villon and Marcel Duchamp, and he took part in the Section d'Or exhibition of 1912 at the Galerie La Boétie, organized by Jacques Villon.

The American artist Arthur Dove spent two years in Europe (1907-1909). He worked for the most part in oils, watercolours and pastels; later, from 1920 on, he devoted himself chiefly to collages. This pastel of 1915, *Plant Forms*, is among the first of his compositions in which abstraction prevails over the highly stylized figural motif. It is the pictorial expression of a dynamic force in concentric movement, built up chiefly in semicircular forms. The vocabulary is almost Cubist, with its definition of a three-dimensional space, the intersecting curves, the transposition of natural motifs into geometric figures. Made up of broad areas of thick pigment with a velvety, lustreless texture, this pastel emphasizes the contrasts between the brighter zones of colour firmly set into a network of dark volutes and outlines. In the energy and intensity of the movement, this picture is akin to the Expressionism of Kandinsky and Franz Marc.

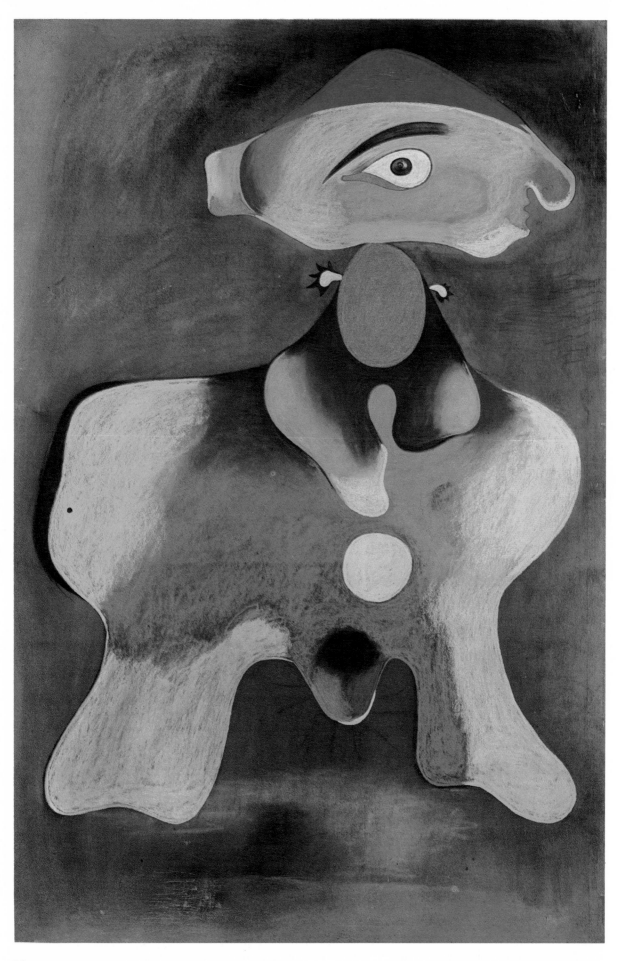

Joan Miró
(1893-1983)
Woman, 1934.
Pastel and pencil on buff paper.

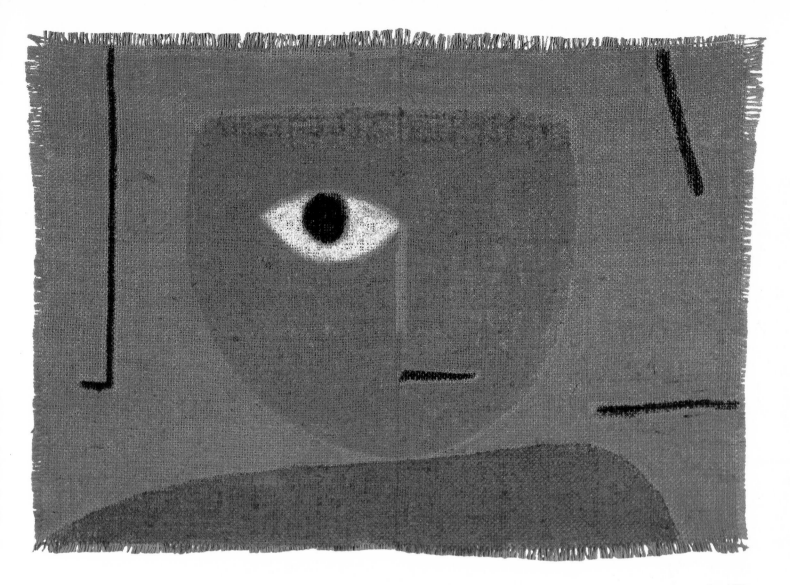

The support or ground plays an essential and singular role in Klee's work, as in *The Eye* of 1938, executed on a strip of jute from a gunny sack, with frayed edges and loose weave, which was then laid over cardboard. The pastel powder was applied to the previously moistened cloth and then quickly absorbed, as if diluted into the thickness of the jute. The result is a thin layer of pigment, allowing the weave to show through and giving a light, airy texture, similar to that of watercolour. The three broad colour surfaces, pink, green and grey, are set off by five black lines and the white patch of the eye.

Signed and dated 1937, Klee's *Oriental Garden* is a reminiscence of his journey to Tunisia, to Kairouan, in 1914, and to Egypt in 1928. It is painted on a close-woven strip of cotton. The black lines conjure up a three-domed palace, a stairway, arcades and trees; these figural elements are laid over a purely geometric pattern of rectangles, squares and triangles, very much like the detail of *Flowering* of 1934 (see page 79), where the bright tints of pastel and their bold juxtapositions were applied directly to the black ground with dry sticks, in broad parallel streaks on the paper ground.

After joining the Surrealist group, Miró developed the art of combining plant, animal and human forms taken from the visible world with a fanciful spawning of abstract or imaginary forms. As he advanced along his chosen path, he came to lay increasing emphasis on cosmic motifs. About 1929 began his calculated breaking-up of figures: this experimental upheaval he himself described as "the assassination of painting."

Dating from 1934, the pastel entitled *Woman* represents a symbolic, ectoplasmic figure hovering in cosmic space, with an oscillating, balloon-like movement, beyond the pull of gravity. Illuminated by sunlight or moonlight coming from the right, the flattened and distorted head looks to the right, in side view. This caricatural, monstrous head, with its over-sized eye, comes as a forerunner of the series of "Wild Paintings" of 1937, in which Miró shattered the human face, in pursuance and fulfilment of his set purpose: "to break away from reality." The buff paper ground, setting off the bright pastel colours, further accentuates the velvety texture and compact thickness of the pigments. Some details of the figure are treated as flat areas of pure colour, others in superimposed colour patches of different tones.

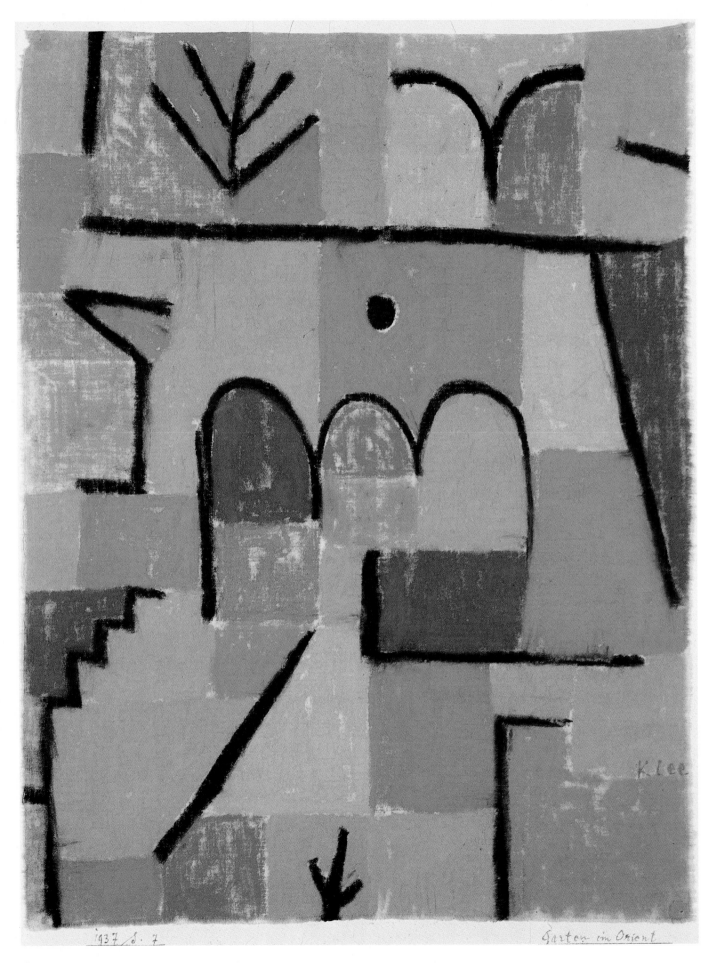

1937 δ. 7   Garten im Orient

Executed in pastel, gouache and Indian ink, *Women and Bird in Front of the Sun* of 1942 makes free play with the new profusion of elements and movements, of rhythms and trajectories, evoking the fourth dimension— a theme, or intimation of a theme, which Miró had been developing in his *Constellations*, a series of gouaches which he had begun in January 1940. These latter were a hymn to the sun, in reaction against the grimness of the war years. They were commented on by Jacques Dupin: ''The artist's mission is to bring happy visions to saddened eyes. He is there to remind us that, in a world transformed by human folly into a battlefield, there will always be stars and birds.'' Here, in *Women and Bird in Front of the Sun*, pastel is used rather as a priming coat, its patches and rubbings and stumpings being then worked over with gouache and Indian ink.

*Ground texture
and mixed media*

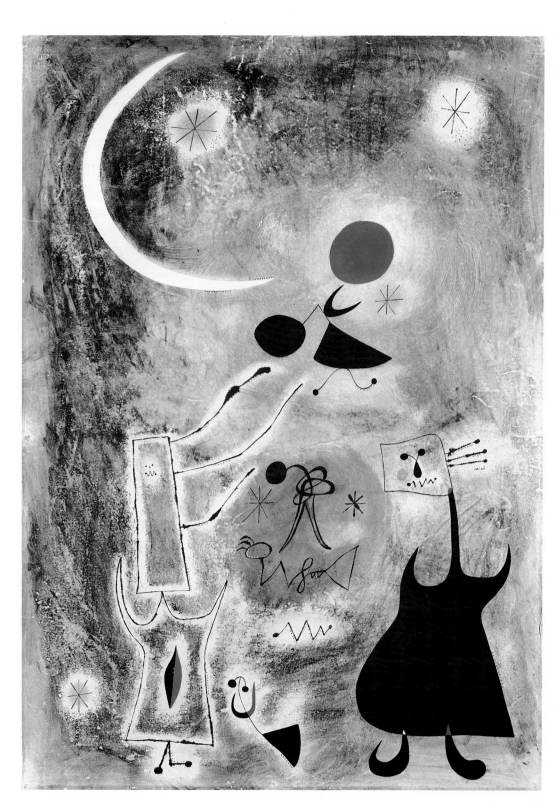

Paul Klee
(1879-1940)
Oriental Garden, 1937.
Pastel on cotton.

Joan Miró
(1893-1983)
Women and Bird in
Front of the Sun, 1942.
Pastel, gouache and
Indian ink on white wove paper.

Sketched out at high speed, Fautrier's light pastel of 1929 is an elliptical notation, evoking a wooded landscape or rather the memory or trace of that landscape, which has already faded, erased by passing time and oblivion. Standing in the forefront of the advance beyond the researches of Impressionism, Fautrier anticipated by a decade or more that imaginary mind-world so searchingly re-explored again, from the 1950s on, by Antoni Tápies and Cy Twombly. With Wols, Fautrier was one of the inventors of Informal art or Tachisme. The central motif, the colour patch or *tache*, no longer corresponds to the representation of a visible object; it simply expresses a colour or texture or cluster of pigments, by an unconstrained play of gesture and involuntary upsurge of shapes and dribbles of paint. "Art is only a medium of exteriorization, but it is a wild medium, without rules or reckonings" (Jean Fautrier). Even in this uncomplicated pastel drawing, one gets an inkling of the work that went into it, from the successive layers and thicknesses of pigment, thrown off

"... a wild medium, without rules or reckonings"

Jean Fautrier
(1898-1964)
Untitled, 1929.
Pastel on cardboard.

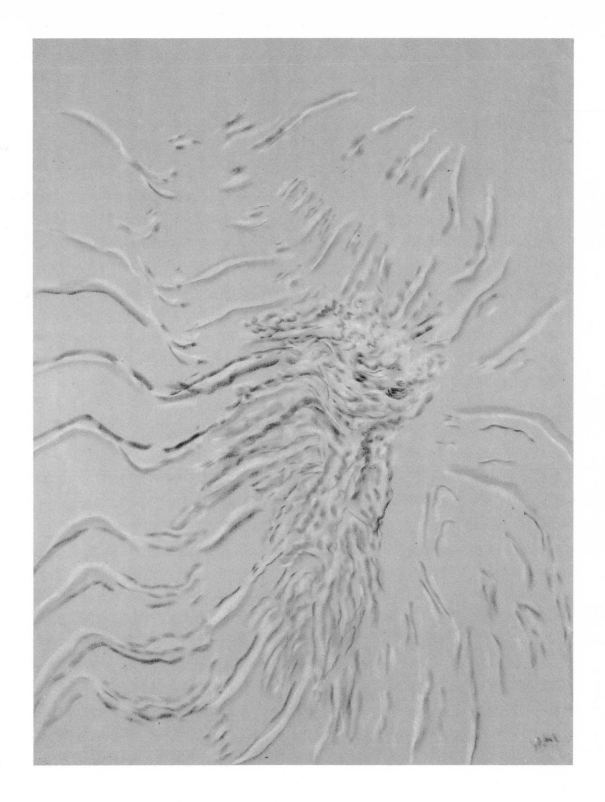

Henri Michaux
(1899)
Untitled, 1964.
Pastel on grey velvet paper.

from the moving hand and interacting with the ground texture, in the centre of which the floating shape seems to hover. The colour patch signifies an element or fragment of nature (landscape, still life or nude).

For Henri Michaux, intent as he was on reaching out to "another reality," the patch of ink or pastel may convey many meanings. As automatic writing it may reveal the depths of the unconscious mind. It may also serve to express ideographic signs. It may contain a suggestion of imagery, bringing to mind this or that object or figure. A face seems to rise up at the centre of this strange, spidery pastel. An apparition? A hallucination? "Faces: one of the realest things for me, yet even there object became subject so easily, reality was wanting, passing away. Rather than lines, their fleetingness came up to me, phantoms of a sponge emotion. Or I went to them, as if to traffic lanes, to courtyards, to fountains, to gardens. Not at all closed up, a face, but criss-crossed, shared out, dissolved and dissolving; or else one runs up against the invisible. And always the eyes remain with lights of another world" (Henri Michaux, *Emergences-Resurgences*, Geneva, 1972).

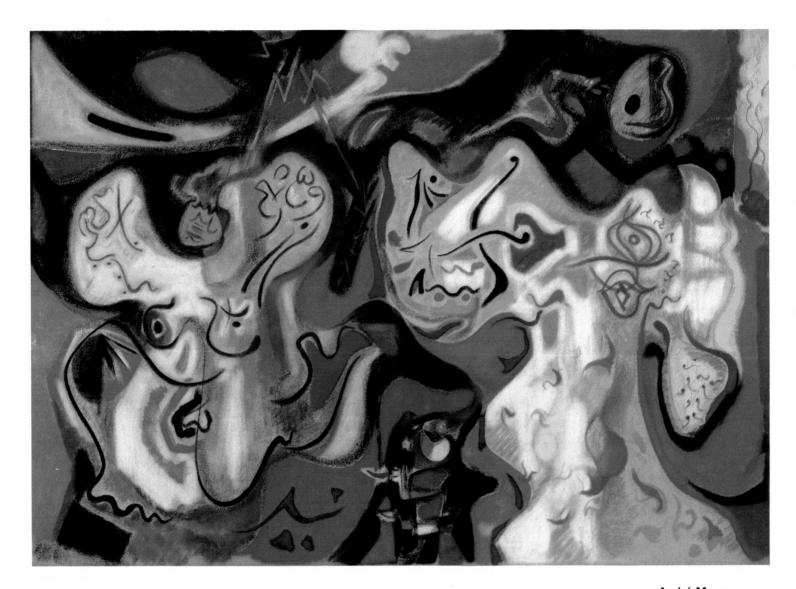

André Masson
(1896)

The Pythia (Priestess
of the Oracle of Apollo), 1943.
Pastel on grey-buff paper.

This untitled pastel of 1964, is all in soft pale tones of white, yellow, blue and pink, some in the faintest touches. The streakings and interlacings of darker tones go to create an illusion of laceration.

Dating from 1943, André Masson's pastel *The Pythia* was executed on grey-buff paper. Beginning about 1925, Masson employed pastels in combination with pencil and coloured crayons. Harmony was no part of his purpose. He sought out rather paroxysmic schemes of acid, clashing blues, violets, reds, yellows; indeed almost all the colours of the palette are there. The theme of Woman possessed of magic powers (here the priestess of the oracle of Apollo at Delphi) and war-making energies is one that recurs repeatedly in his work, usually in the shape of a giant figure extending to the full height and breadth of the picture

space. This gestural power is characteristic of all the themes in which Masson, in a frenzied tangle of broken lines, expresses death, violence, brute force: *Massacres* (1931-1933) and *Sacrifices* (1934), where the composition all but overflows the surface of the sheet. *The Pythia* was painted during Masson's American exile, in New England, from 1941 to 1945. "Impelled by the terrestrial force and climatic extremes of this region, where we settled for four years, I sought out and perhaps found some pictorial equivalents of these elemental forces. Telluric mysteries. Phenomena of hatching and germination thus found their transposition in many canvases and pastels" (André Masson, in Jean-Paul Clébert, *Mythologie d'André Masson*, Geneva, 1971). Line only partly corresponds to contours. It serves rather to mark out certain colour fields which combine and clash in accordance with a pendulum rhythm acting throughout the sheet and heightening the sense of instability. Over the colour fields is superimposed a governing pattern of curves, signs, zigzags, strokes and hatchings.

This untitled work by Pollock, of 1945-1946, was executed in a wide variety of mixed media (brush and spatter, pen, black and coloured inks, pastel, gouache and wash on paper). From about 1945 on, Pollock used his "all-over" technique to create a homogeneous surface, without a single climax, every part receiving equal emphasis. The representational elements became less and less recognizable, till they vanished in an intricate pattern stemming ultimately from Surrealist abstraction. The style of Jackson Pollock and that of André Masson were closely akin in 1945. Both had worked in New York in S.W. Hayter's Atelier 17: Masson from 1941 to 1945, Pollock from the autumn of 1944 to the summer of 1945 (William Rubin, *Notes on Masson and Pollock,* New York, 1959). The profiled silhouettes, the interrupted

lines, the dynamics, the pendulum movements, the all-over shattering of forms: these were common to both men. Figuration is even less perceptible in Pollock. Lines break off into diagonals, brief parallel hatchings, patches, splashes, nets and skeins of paint, creating the illusion of depth and the fourth dimension. Pastel intervenes in coloured accents independently of contours and is then sometimes worked over in Indian ink. These are not so much accents as "coloured fields," to use the expression of Masson. The years 1945-1946 were for Pollock a transitional period between paintings still possessing recognizable signs (faces, skeletons, fish, arrows), convulsed by a centrifugal movement, and paintings of a purely gestural abstraction. This untitled picture in mixed media anticipates the invention of the drip technique, which really began in 1947. Line is the expression of inner passion, of an instability and violence flaring outwards in an intricately tangled reflection of the artist's emotional drives.

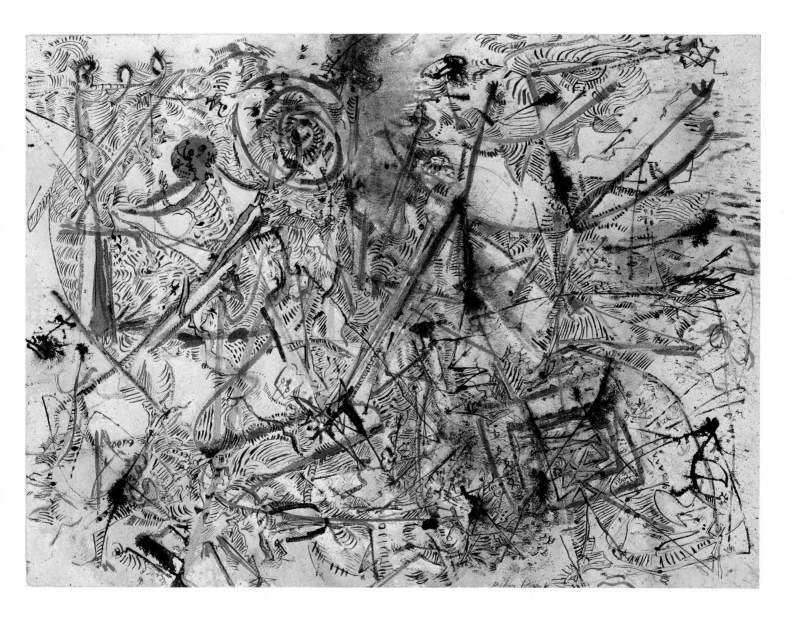

Jackson Pollock
(1912-1956)
Untitled, 1945-1946.
Brush and spatter, pen, black and coloured inks, pastel, gouache and wash on paper.

91

Gorky's *Summation* of 1947, a pencil, pastel and charcoal drawing on buff paper, achieves a synthesis between pure, supple, harmonious and indeed flawless linework, on the one hand, and, on the other, automatic writing at its most spontaneous and imaginative. Line goes to define forms, while colour underscores certain accents: patches, shadows, circles, stumpings, rubbings.

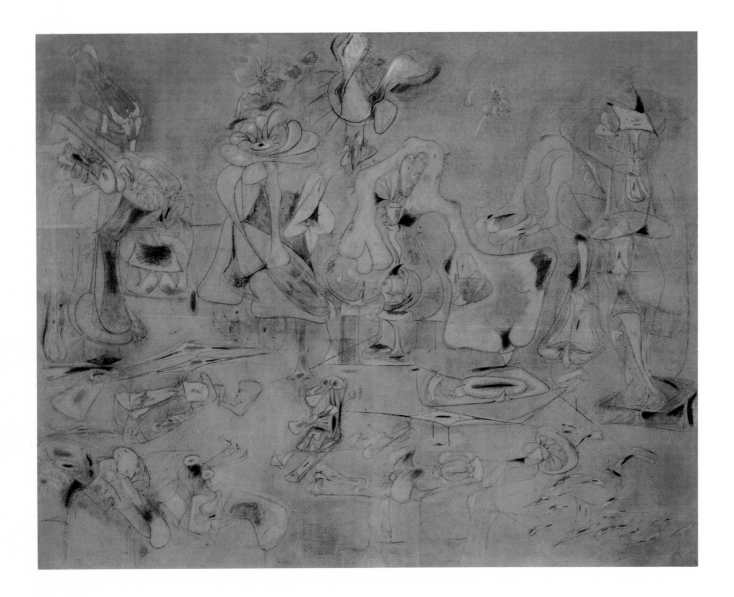

A continuous narration unfolds in the form of a story, as a frieze and ellipse, running parallel to the picture surface. The composite figures, born of free-flowing fancy, are put together in a thoroughly surrealistic spirit. The eclecticism of Gorky's style is an echo of the interacting influences of his closest friends, Willem de Kooning, Miró and Matta; the latter two he met in New York in the early 1940s.

Matta's growing influence on Gorky can be detected in several coloured crayon drawings of 1943, which unfold however in a more continuous and linear manner. But the conception of space is quite different in Matta; with him, forms remain suspended in space in a whirling cosmic movement. Gorky's inspiration took its momentum from naturalistic elements, "Of all the Surrealist artists, Gorky was the only one who maintained direct contact with nature" (André Breton).

Arshile Gorky
(1904-1948)
Summation, 1947.
Pencil, pastel and charcoal
on buff paper.

92

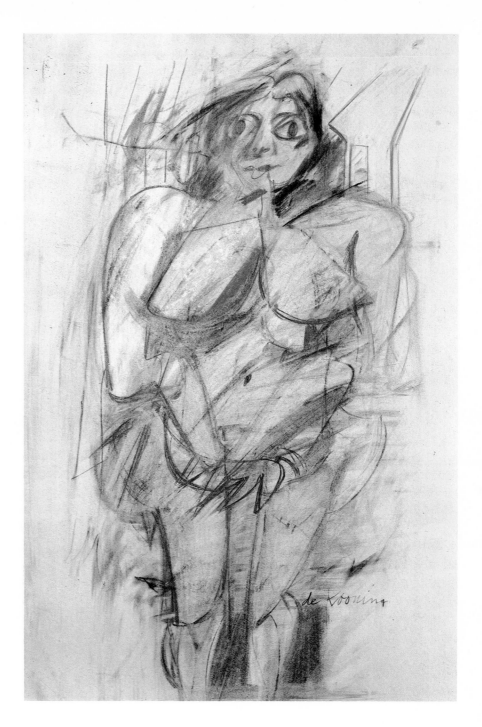

Willem de Kooning
(1904)
Woman, 1952.
Pastel and pencil.

Shortly after emigrating from Holland to the United States in 1926, de Kooning became friendly with Gorky and came under the influence of Surrealism. By 1948 he was seen rather as an abstract artist, even though figural representation remained strong. The overlaid and interwoven lines, bringing forth forms and curves like multiple layers of pentimenti, may be a lingering echo of Cubism.

The pastel of de Kooning's *Woman* is applied very lightly, mingling with the spirited pencil strokes, which are effaced, stumped and then repeated, thus barring the figure with several diagonals. Line with him is always an expression of essentials: it sets the level of emphasis and dynamism of figure attitudes. Bursting with vitality, these imposing silhouettes have haunting faces and over-large eyes.

The staple of de Kooning's work is the human form, more accurately the female body seen in front view, usually in an incomplete or truncated presentation, not far removed from the traditional vision of man, but marked by the heritage of Cubism. His attachment to classical figuration has its source in the thorough academic schooling he received in his early years in Rotterdam. Sometimes the body is headless, an effective device for bringing out with arresting directness the unreality of these schematized, geometrized figures. Paradoxically, the image conveyed is that of a timeless idol. De Kooning achieved a synthesis of his own between abstraction and figuration, with a play of line as free as that of Masson or Pollock. Forms and colours are stepped up to an equivalent intensity, though he often subsides into a suaver scale of pinks, yellows and blues.

Done in 1950, at the same time as an unpublished series of illustrations for Pablo Neruda's poems, this pastel is entitled *El hombre es la zoologia historica*. One of Matta's most personal inventions was this dreamlike futuristic space in which beings of his own devising, half-man, half-machine, move at the speed of light in a science-fiction atmosphere. The wealth of colours extends over an infinite range of modulations. Pastel is geared to

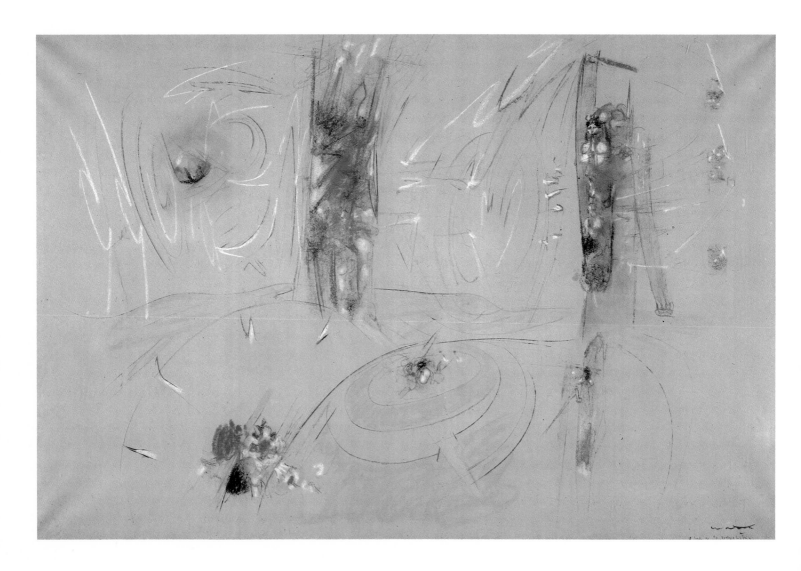

the triple expression of an almost symphonic manner of evoking the void, an intense display of colour enriched by overlaid pigments, a blurred and phosphorescent texture. Each work by Matta is inhabited by these cosmic figures, turning in circular rhythms or speeding on diagonal trajectories of unlimited implications.

Chilean-born and schooled in Paris, Matta was in New York during the war. There, in 1942, he met Marcel Duchamp, who said of him: "His first and major contribution to Surrealist painting was the discovery of hitherto unexplored realms of space in the domain of art. Matta followed modern physicists in the search for a new space which, though represented on canvas, should not be taken for another illusion of the third dimension."

His stumped and rubbed pastels were always light and supple in these years 1950-1952, proceeding by the juxtaposition of outlined elements and still close in spirit to the "tinting" of his coloured crayon drawings of 1942.

Roberto Matta Echaurren
(1911)
El hombre es la zoologia
historica, 1950.
Pastel on buff paper.

94

Lam's *Bird Woman*, dated 1965, is a pastel forming part of a series of half-length fetish-women, hybrid creatures stemming from an imaginary world whose sources lie both in primitive art and in the ritual of magic ceremonies inspired by voodoo cults. In this artist, a Cuban of mixed Chinese and African extraction, we find the instinctual drive of the true primitive.

This accounts for the uninhibited combination of animal and

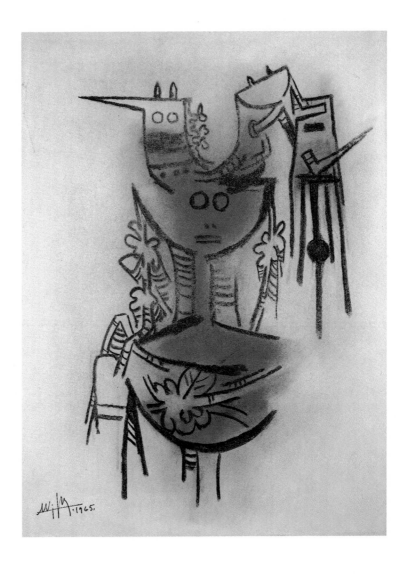

human forms, together with the creation of hybrid monsters, half-bird, half-human. Characteristic of Lam's painting, met with again and again, are figures soaring through the air. Here the muted colour harmony, contained by thick black outlines, is based on red, yellow and carmine. Colour was laid in to begin with over broad areas which were then reworked with black strokes of unerring sureness, forming a pattern through which the powdery pastel glows. The latter intervenes as a kind of halo of shifting ruddy colour, pulsing under and over the black lines broken by sharp angles. This austere geometry and play of divergent planes in space undoubtedly has its source in the African woodcarvings which Lam discovered as a student in Madrid in 1923.

This *Bird Woman* adorned with a sceptre, her necklaces bristling with knives, is thus perceived as a disquieting divinity, combining human power and animal power thanks to this embodied bird, symbol of the soul and the soarings of the mind.

Wifredo Lam
(1902-1982)
Bird Woman, 1965.
Pastel on buff paper.

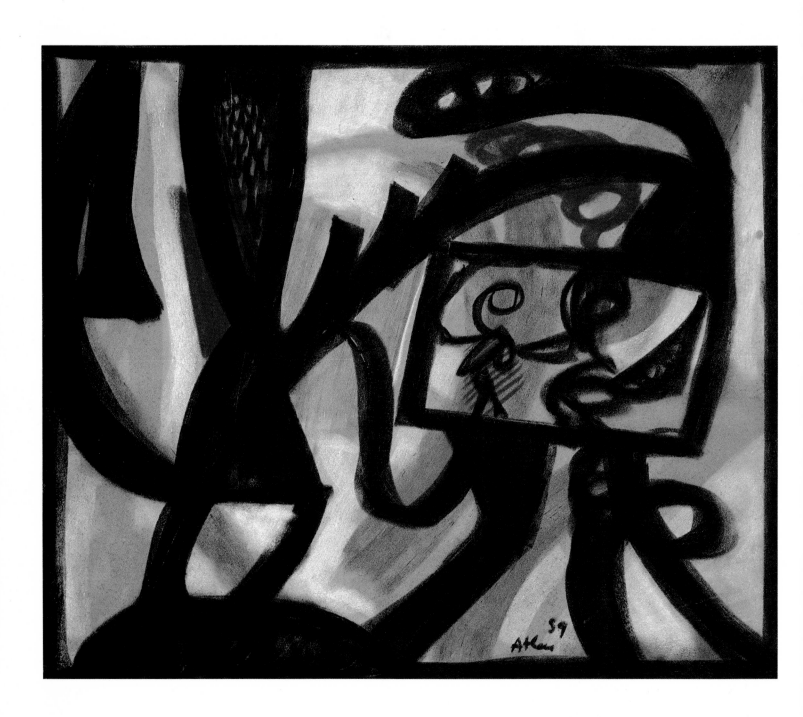

This pastel by Atlan is painted in broad sweeps of black and colour, making the most of the grain of the velvet paper; the latter reinforces the textural effect obtained by the overlaying of deep-toned, reverberant colours. The black strokes define the contours in supple volutes whose abstract forms enclose the spaces reserved for the colours and unwind like wind-buffeted streamers. A dynamic equilibrium is achieved between the intensity of the blacks and the éclat of colour pigments at their purest.

Atlan aimed at a synthesis between a symbolic signwork and an abstract signwork deriving from Moslem calligraphy, a source he owed to his dual heritage as a Jew and a North African. Each of his pictures is built up from a well-constructed drawing, forcibly structured by black, "petrified" outlines. The essential thing for him was rhythm: "I paint mostly with my arms. I yield to the same impulses that a dancer yields to." Actually his work stands on the borderline between abstract schematism and figural representation, between automatic writing and gestural expressionism. This and other late pastels, built up in layers of pigment, were done in the French countryside of the Yonne department, during a period of concentrated output in November-December 1959, before his premature death in February 1960. Atlan stands out as one of the foremost Abstract Expressionists in Europe.

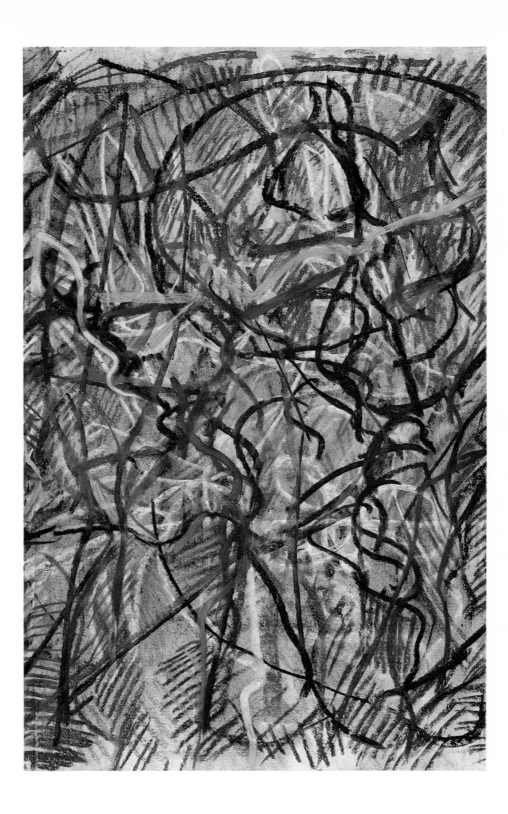

Jean Atlan
(1913-1960)
Untitled, 1959.
Pastel on velvet paper.

Jean-Paul Riopelle
(1924)
Untitled, 1968.
Pastel.

Built up with hatchings, then worked over in a vibrant pattern of interlacing lines, this Riopelle pastel of 1968 is structured by moving curves continually overlaying the initial network of streaks. The ever multiplying lines create an oscillating movement on the picture surface. This vigorous rhythm is generated by decisive gestures which, brought home with energy and vehemence, project a rich store of impulses and sensations. There are signs of erasures and afterthoughts, but this is no longer the automatism of the Surrealists. As Riopelle explains: "Automatic writing is part of an intellectual climate. True automatism would have to occur outside the individual. Wherever there is gesture, it is always guided by the individual. There is no such thing as automatism... The essential thing is intensity." After being close to the American Abstract Expressionists, such as Franz Kline and Willem de Kooning, Riopelle left his native Canada and settled in France in 1946. He then evolved towards the expression of an untrammelled spontaneity. Whatever the final appearance of his works, whether abstract-looking or figural-seeming, a close connection with nature is always present in strength. This pastel with its endless skein of sweeping, undulating lines is suggestive of the pattern of earth and sky as seen from an aircraft (Riopelle himself is a pilot).

In the mental and mathematical world of diagrams, pastel has been resorted to for lines of different colours serving to determine with almost algebraic accuracy a span of time or an extent of space. Plotted lines, curves, diagonals and vectors become the expression of conceptual thought, and no longer that of a gesture or a practical technique. For Arakawa line has many functions. It may serve to set the scale of size, to measure and delimit certain fields of space (their surface or their edge), to define the superimposition of geometric volumes, to establish connections and sequences, to outline colour networks, to indicate a vanishing point or to designate a shifting of volume. Arrows and vectors trace out movements of rotation. Proceeding on continuous trajectories or broken off by dotted lines, going off into zigzags, diagonals or narrowing or sweeping curves, the different coloured lines criss-cross and carve out various visual and semantic fields. Not one axis but several are suggested —axes of symmetry, of rotation, of oscillation. The starting point of this working out of Arakawa's thought processes is an extreme development of the artist's sensibility and visual acuity, enabling him to achieve the utmost objectivity of perception. The successive stages of this process might be described as feeling, thinking, naming. And in fact lettering, words and statements play a key part in these pastels. They appear in letters and script continually varying in size, colour, intensity and gradation. In some works they may be read from the top downwards, in others from the bottom upwards or from right to left. They are laid in over lines, numbers and objects.

In *The Call of Continuity*, as in other compositions of these years 1975-1980, an off-centre vertical axis delimits the section opposing solid and void. The notion of the Void (nothingness, emptiness, vacuum, tabula rasa...) is one of the fundamental concepts of Arakawa's work: it is what he calls the Blank. Among the words in capital letters inscribed on the left and relating to movements, forms, volumes and sounds, some of them seem to provide the makings of a poem: drift, spin, shifting, texture, breath, blue.

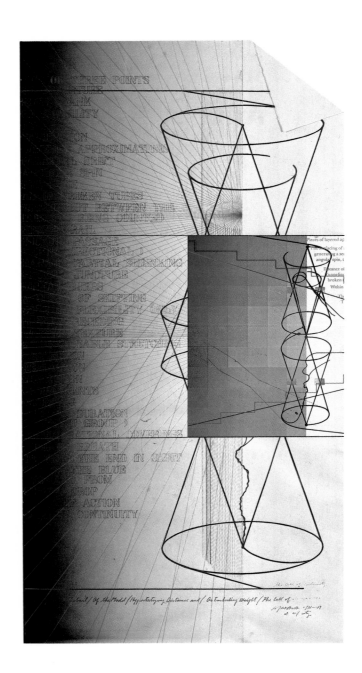

Shusaku Arakawa
(1936)
The Call of Continuity, 1980.
Pastel, pencil and silkscreen
collage on buff paper.

As with Arakawa, the essential thrust of Patrick Naggar's mind-pictures bears on the dual purpose of his artistic handwriting: its meaning and its direction. Its implications unfold in letters progressing from left to right or from right to left, readable right side up or upside down, and at times only to be deciphered with the help of a mirror, by way of reminding the viewer of the reversibil-

Patrick Naggar
(1946)
Diagram, 1982.
Pastel on paper.

ity of every form integrated into the cosmos. Letters and numbers raise questions about the terms and relations of the new measurement of time, memory and space. For Naggar, who is both architect and painter, pastel is a privileged medium present in most of his projects. In this *Diagram*, drawn directly without any outside element, graduated lines in all four margins indicate the scale of size. These geometric divisions, abscissae and ordinates, plot out the frame of reference for an intricate signwork suggesting the remnants of a lost alphabet, its now illegible letters laid bare pell-mell in successive strata, like vestiges of an age-old

civilization. It is like a resurrected page from a buried book of spells or a manuscript palimpsest full of indecipherable hieroglyphs, some showing through, some half blurred or effaced. There is no hierarchy here in the concept of writing and lettering. What we have is an artist's meditation on the course taken by human writing, with all its intimations of spontaneous or automatic gestures and its pentimenti. The intervention of light and the study of its variable intensities is a permanent line of research in Naggar's work (paintings, architectural designs, environments, decorations).

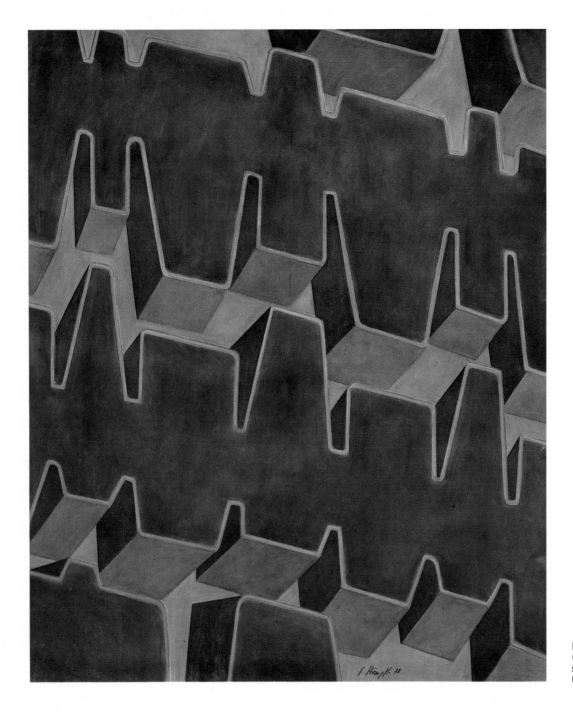

Peter Stämpfli
(1937)
Sempione, 1980.
Pastel.

Peter Stämpfli's pastels, with their varying system of interlocking planes, follow up motifs deriving from Photo Realism and Pop Art and handled in a style that owes much to photography, billboard advertising and comic strips. The image consists of sharply patterned lines standing out from a colour background. Each form is repeated in parallel rows and endless series, designed to dovetail. The bold cut-off and head-on focus thrust the enlarged detail forward with an unavoidable impact. Size is the keynote, the motifs being blown up and thereby distorted till all sense of scale is lost. Some studies based originally on the tread and cracking of a rubber tire take on an illusory gigantism suggesting a monumental close-up of clefts or rifts.

It was in 1971 that Stämpfli began focusing his eye on tire treads. In 1974 he started working from blown-up film strips. As for his remarkable series of pastels, it developed and unfolded essentially from 1979 to 1982. He used pastel for its areas of intense colour and its covering thickness. The side illumination of a raking light emphasizes the articulation of forms and each of their facets. Beginning with a realistic representation, he evolved towards abstraction, towards a reductionist vision to which is added the idea of imprints, traces, memories. With Stämpfli, as with Titus-Carmel, the work is not conceived as a self-contained item but as one of a series.

Begun in 1980 and continued throughout the year 1981, Titus-Carmel's sequence of *Caparisons* consists of thirteen variants executed in red chalk, pencil, pen and ink, watercolour and pastel. All are based on the same form, built up with rigorous symmetry and by its intense, abiding presence suggesting the idea of a medieval ornament, a shield or breastplate or heavy curtain adorned with fringes.

Elements of a transposed reality

"Almost by chance," writes Titus-Carmel, describing the origin of this sequence, "a funerary caparison, with its wrought silver beading, somehow landed in my studio." The only pastel of the series, this painting is executed in a broad, easy, flexible manner, with fine stripes laid across it in a scale of deep-toned colours, grey, blue, violet, green, discreetly set off by yellow. Breadth of execution distinguishes each work of the series, all of them in a monumental style of almost outdoor freshness: one feels the impact of a buffeting wind against this streaming curtain of rain. Completed on 10 October 1981, the sequence of *Caparisons* is in perfect harmony with the autumn colours of nature: "Ochres of the dying year. Sinuous mottlings, muffled purples: and so I make my bow to this mourning cloth, to the rustle of dead leaves and the flow of waters reflecting faded autumn gold."

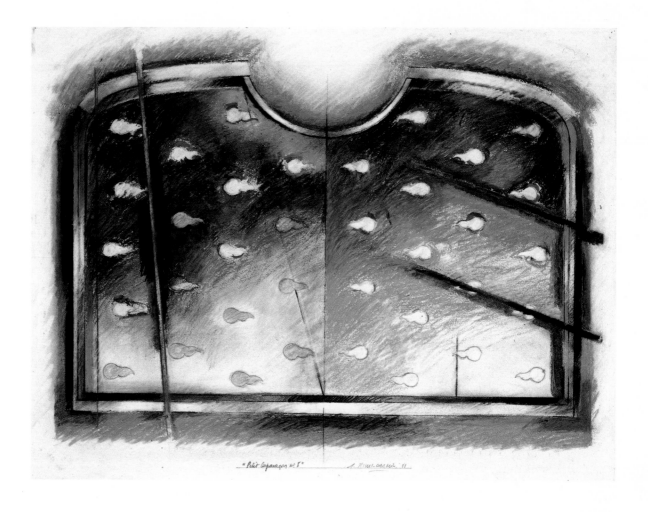

Gérard Titus-Carmel
(1942)
Small Caparison No. 1, 1981.
Pastel.

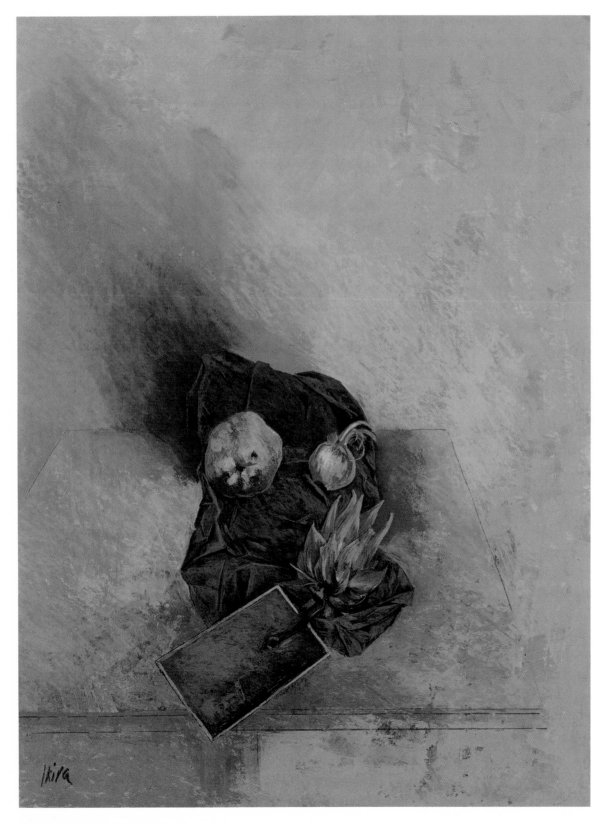

Pierre Skira
(1938)
Still Life, 1983.
Pastel.

Return to the pastellist's craft and practice

The return to representational painting was part of a broad movement whose sources go back to the late 1950s, to the inventions of Pop Art and its over-sized images in close-up, caught at odd angles of focus or along a plunging line of sight and thrown forward in bright colours. Reinstating the figural image and even the actual presence of objects, this powerful trend grew fast and enjoyed a spectacular development, both in England (R.B. Kitaj, Allen Jones, David Hockney) and the United States (Jasper Johns, Robert Rauschenberg, Andy Warhol, Roy Lichtenstein, Claes Oldenburg, James Rosenquist, Tom Wesselmann, George Segal, Jim Dine). It arose in reaction against Abstract Expressionism, but without exactly repudiating it. With Anglo-American Pop Art setting the pace, related movements, less forceful however, arose in France and Italy —New Realism, for example. Since then, other figural movements have developed more in the direction of a neo-classicism stimulated by the recent rediscovery of nineteenth-century academic painting.

This return to the past answers in part to the need felt by many artists of today to re-learn and re-master traditional techniques and workmanship. Among them, active now for nearly twenty years, is a new generation of painters keenly and indeed almost exclusively interested in the pastel medium. Some of the best known are Sam Szafran, Pierre Skira and François Barbâtre. The return to figural imagery has brought with it a renewed interest in still life, focused on everyday objects, on studio gear, on kitchen utensils and food. Such is the silent world of Pierre Skira's pastels, drawn with unerring precision and concentrated on a very few objects punctuating a table top or a shelf. The combination of objects, bringing together the tools of the studio and food supplies from the neighbourhood market, is apt to be unexpected: an artichoke, an onion, a lithographic stone, a coal bucket and so on.

With a deliberate and effective use of schematic patterning, François Barbâtre resorts to the close-up, in the manner of the Photo Realists, setting it off by the sharp recession of vanishing lines and an adroit distortion of each of the space-defining elements. Here the angle of sight is set low, nearly at floor level, between two looming portfolios of drawings which open the perspective. The colour harmony is unusual for its acidity: violet, pink, red, absinth green.

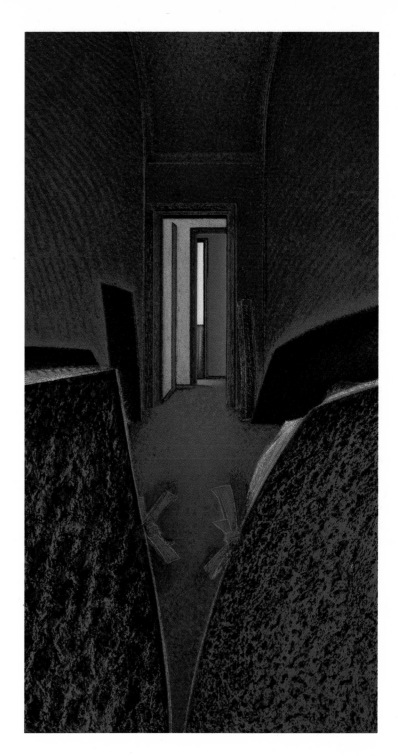

François Barbâtre
(1938)
The Corridor, 1982.
Pastel on paper.

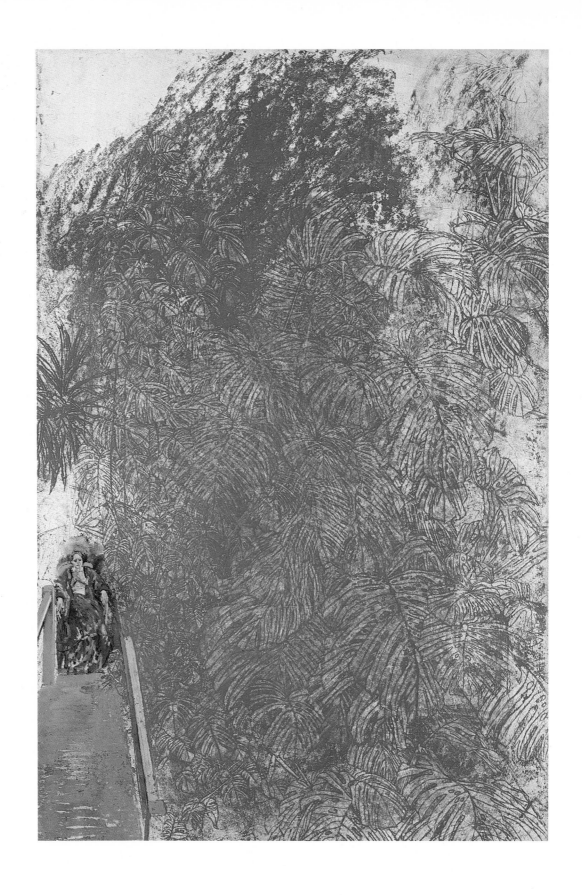

Sam Szafran
(1934)
Greenhouse, 1974.
Pastel.
Studio, 1972.
Pastel.

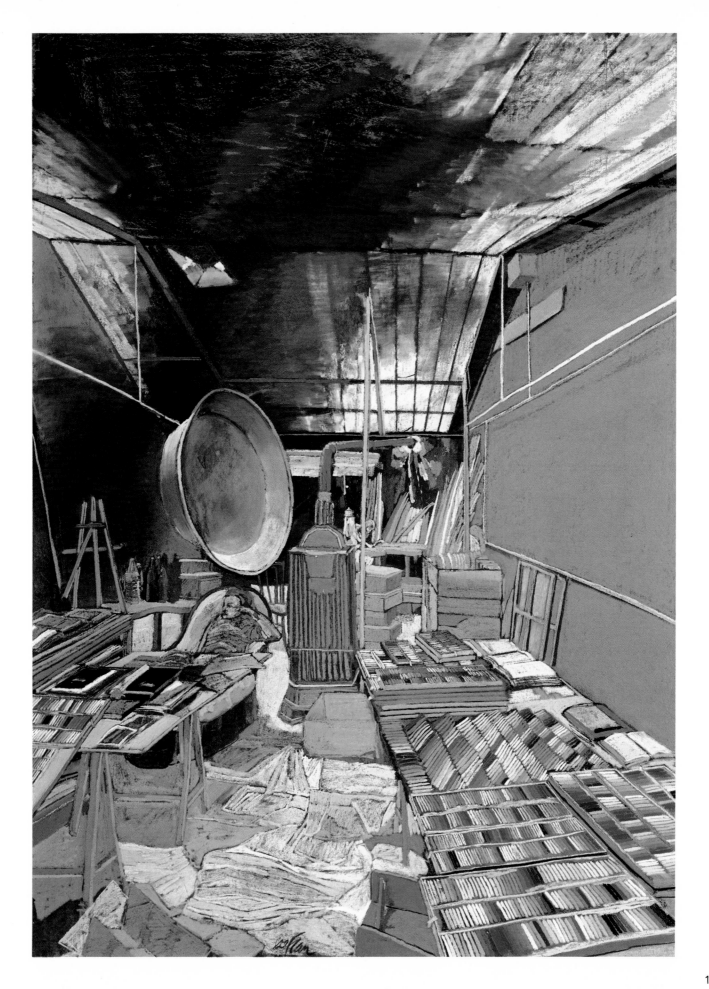

The themes Sam Szafran is most fond of, continually returning to them and varying them, are the greenhouse, the stairs and the interior of his studio (overall views, corridor perspectives, shelves, ceiling beams, details of open boxes containing pastel sticks of all different colours). For each of these themes he uses a slightly differentiated perspective system, making play with a varying scale of distortions of the picture space. In the series of *Plants* or *Greenhouses* the masses of leafage tower up in the foreground, running parallel to the picture plane, in a succession of frontal motifs. The blue (that is, the abstract) leaves alternate in an opaque or transparent mass, only their contours being accurately outlined. To draw these leaves Szafran used two sheets of paper. On the first, previously covered on the back with a thick coat of ultramarine blue cobalt pastel, he laid in on the front the incisive contours which were printed off on the definitive support placed underneath.

The isolated figure of a man or woman, constituting the "figure scene," is relegated to the edge of the composition and seen from a distance, as if through a field-glass, in accordance with a trick perspective combining the close-up and the far-away in juxtaposition and contrast.

In the *Studio* the perspective system is much more traditional. Compact and thick, applied in successive layers, the pastel pigments are unified over the whole surface of the picture. As for the *Stairway* theme, which made its appearance in 1974, Szafran developed it in a long series of distorted views, suggestive of an anamorphosis and comparable to the views obtained from a curving mirror. They seem to stem from a sensation of giddy descent. They convey the oscillations of an artist seeking to determine his own field of vision —akin to that of a sculptor— and to single out the most representative axis, the significant detail: the shape of each step, the rise and flight of the stairs, the labyrinthine spiral of the stair-well, the distortion of the bay-windows, the lurking shadows of a landing.

All these off-centre visions, with their sense of a precarious balance, fraught with the lure of the abyss and the desire to baffle pursuit, were drawn from the sixth-floor lodgings in the Rue de Seine, Paris, where the poet Fouad El-Etr lives, one of the artist's closest friends. After long watching Szafran at work, Fouad wrote him in 1974 a series of letters which he entitled "Outline of a Treatise on Pastels": "It is enough for me to look on with apprehension at this geological frenzy, this slow and methodical endeavour to set things down, like a tide of pollen over a wild flower or a cluster of powder on a butterfly's wing."

Many artists of today are eagerly exploring the possibilities of pastel, which they use either in addition to other media or with a special preference. Among them are Michael Bastow, Olivier O. Olivier, Irving Petlin, Antonio Segui and Ferdinando Botero, all figure painters; Piero Guccione, Martial Raysse and Joerg Ortner, who are chiefly landscapists. Other styles, other themes, have also found apt expression in pastels: the abstract lyricism of Joan Mitchell, the serial and imaginative experiments of Christian Fossier, Alfred Hofkunst, Jacques Poli and Daniel Pommereulle.

Pastel,
a technique of
yesterday and today

The recipe for making pastel sticks intended for painters was given by several early writers. Artists made them themselves according to their own requirements.

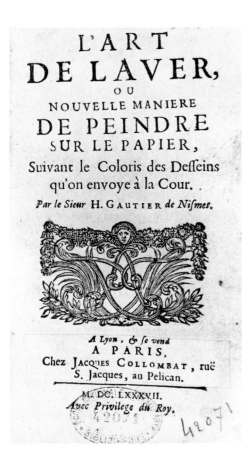

A very old pastel recipe was given by Petrus Gregorius in *Syntaxeon Artis mirabilis*, Cologne, 1583.

"Secret found out by Monsieur Le Prince Robert," from H. Gautier de Nismes, *L'Art de laver...* ("The Art of wash-drawing or new manner of painting on paper"), Paris, 1687.

Take some white clay, as prepared for making tobacco pipes, and using ordinary water knead it with ground porphyry or shell, till you get a paste. And take some colours, each one separately, and grind them dry on the finest-grained stone you can find, then strain them through taffeta or very fine linen cloth, and mix each colour with this paste, according as you wish the paste more or less tinted. Add to it a little ordinary honey and water of gum arabic at discretion. Some paste for each colour must be darker and some less dark, in order to make the lights and shades. Then take each of your pastes, and make rolls of them as big as your finger, rolling them between two smooth boards or on paper in the shade for two days; then, to dry them out, they should be exposed to sunlight or the fire, and being dry will be used with satisfaction.

"Secret found out by Monsieur Le Prince Robert," from *Secrets concernant les arts et métiers* ("Secrets concerning the arts and crafts"), Brussels, 1766.

Painters fashion these coloured crayons in the form of a cylinder and roll them with a mixture of fish glue, gum arabic, fig juice or, what I think is better, whey. The crayons are thereby made softer; otherwise they are hard and scratch the paper.

Of all crayons, those I have just named are the only ones that are natural. But since there are several others which are artificial, and of every sort of colour, all are to be kept in the same order for the composition.
Suppose we want some for making the reds. I then consider whether the colour red carries its gum or not. If it carries its gum, I don't use any water mixed with gum, but water alone. And if it doesn't carry any gum, I use water only slightly mixed with gum. To make the crayon I now take some cinnabar. I have some water mixed with

gum and, on the other side, some white-lead and some very white plaster. I grind all this together, and I fashion some small sticks of colour which I use for drawing just as I use the lead pencil and the red crayon. Practice should give proficiency to those who are willing to use these strong crayons. For they are usually made too soft, and thus wearing down too easily they are no good for drawing with; or else, being too hard if the water is mixed with too much gum, they cannot be made to mark.
The remedy for these defects is to grind them yet again on marble, adding water mixed with gum if they are too soft, or putting in more colour and increasing the composition if they are too hard. And lastly, if the crayons are too faint and have not enough colour in them, let more be added in order to bring them up to the tone that you desire.

Twelve pages from the famous anonymous
"Treatise on Pastel Painting," Paris, 1788.

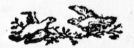

TRAITÉ
DE LA
PEINTURE
AU PASTEL,

Du secret d'en composer les crayons, & des
moyens de le fixer ; avec l'indication d'un grand
nombre de nouvelles substances propres à la
Peinture à l'huile, & les moyens de prévenir
l'altération des couleurs.

Par M. P. R. de C.... C. à P. de L.

Quand on a chez soi de pareils Artistes,
Il n'en faut pas aller chercher ailleurs.
CAVAL. BERNIN.

A PARIS,
Chez DEFER DE MAISONNEUVE, Libraire,
rue du Foin Saint-Jacques, Hôtel
de la Reine Blanche.

Avec Approbation & Privilége du Roi.
1 7 8 8.

TRAITÉ

DE LA

PEINTURE AU PASTEL.

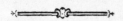

1. LA peinture au paſtel eſt l'art de repréſenter les objets ſur une ſurface plane avec des pâtes compoſées de ſubſtances colorées, qu'on a broyées à l'eau pure & qu'on a fait ſécher après les avoir roulées en forme de crayons.

2. Ce genre de Peinture eſt d'une facilité particulière. Il joint à cet avantage, celui de ne ré-

A v

pandre aucune odeur, de n'oc-caſionner aucune malpropreté, de pouvoir être interrompu quand on veut & repris de même, enfin de ſe prêter à toutes les poſitions, de quelque côté que vienne la lumière.

3. La Peinture au paſtel ſeroit donc généralement préférée, ſur-tout pour le portrait, où l'on eſt ſouvent obligé d'opérer à diffé-rentes repriſes; mais elle n'a, pour ainſi dire, qu'une exiſtence pré-caire, faute de conſiſtance & de ſolidité; la moindre ſecouſſe fait tomber le paſtel : le plus léger frot-tement l'emporte. Il faut, pour le garantir, couvrir les tableaux d'un verre qui court lui-même les plus grands riſques au moindre choc.

4. Cet inconvénient l'a fait né-gliger par les grands Artiſtes. Ils

1. Pastel painting is the art of re-presenting objects on a plane surface with pastes composed of coloured substances, which have been ground in pure water and dried, after being rolled into the shape of crayons.

2. This kind of Painting is par-ticularly easy. To this advantage it adds that of giving off no odour, of occasioning no untidiness; it can be left off whenever one likes and re-sumed again; lastly, it lends itself to any location, from whatever side the light may come.

3. Pastel Painting would there-fore be generally preferred, espe-cially for the portrait, where one is often obliged to take up the work again and again. But it has, so to speak, only a precarious existence, for want of firmness and solidity. The least shaking makes the pastel fall away; the slightest rubbing car-ries it off. By way of safeguard, the pictures have to be covered with glass, which itself runs the greatest risks from the least shock.

4. Because of this inconvenience it has been neglected by the great

ont préféré la Peinture à l'huile, comme plus propre à transmettre leurs ouvrages à la postérité.

5. Cependant on pouvoit trouver un moyen de lui donner aussi de la consistance, en assurant & fixant le pastel. Mais il falloit que les Sçavans tournassent les yeux du côté des Arts, ou que les Artistes les tournassent du côté des sciences.

6. Dans la classe de ceux-ci, M. Loriot, méchanicien de réputation, fit des tentatives assez heureuses en 1753. Mais il se réserva son secret, même après avoir obtenu des marques de la munificence du Gouvernement. Ce n'est qu'en 1780 qu'il l'a publié. Nous y reviendrons bientôt.

7. Dans la classe des autres, M. le Prince de San-Severo di San-

A vj

gro, que Naples doit compter à la fois parmi les Amateurs & les Physiciens les plus recommandables qu'elle ait vu naître, y parvint aussi dans le même tems ; il ne fit aucune difficulté de communiquer le moyen qu'il employoit à M. de la Lande, pendant le voyage que celui-ci fit en Italie en 1766, & qui ne tarda pas à le publier dans sa relation (1). Mais il ne paroît pas qu'on en ait fait grand usage, quoiqu'on le trouve copié dans l'Encyclopédie, & qu'il réussisse très-bien dans de petits tableaux. Nous en parlerons aussi dans la suite, lorsque nous indiquerons les moyens que nous avons trouvés de fixer le pastel en grand ; peut-être que désormais, rien n'empêchera les Artistes de se familiariser avec ce

_____

(1) Voyage d'un François en Italie, tome 6, pag. 398.

Artists. They have preferred oil Painting, as better able to transmit their works to posterity.

5. Some method could however have been found to give it a like firmness, by securing and fixing the pastel. But for that the Scientists would have had to turn their eyes in the direction of the Arts, or the Artists turn them in the direction of the sciences.

6. In the class of those, Monsieur Loriot, a mechanic of repute, made some fairly successful experiments in 1753. But he kept his secret to himself, even after obtaining some tokens of munificence from the Government. It was not till 1780 that he published it. We shall revert to this presently.

7. In the class of the others, the Prince of San Severo di Sangro, whom Naples must count at once among the most commendable Art Lovers and Natural Philosophers to be born there, also achieved it at the same time. He made no objection to communicating the means that he employed to Monsieur de la Lande, during the latter's journey to Italy in 1766, and he published it in his account ("Journey of a Frenchman to Italy," volume 6, page 398). But no great use appears to have been made of it, though one finds it recorded in the Encyclopaedia and it has succeeded very well in small pictures. We shall speak of it subsequently, when we shall indicate the ways that we have found of fixing pastel in large sizes. It may be that henceforth nothing will prevent Artists from

genre de Peinture aimable & facile.

8. Aucun autre n'approche autant de la nature. Aucun ne produit des tons si vrais. C'est de la chair, c'est Flore, c'est l'Aurore. S'il n'a pas quelquefois autant de force que la Peinture à l'huile, c'est moins sa faute que celle de la main qui l'employe.

9. Non que je prétende inviter à quitter le pinceau pour le pastel. Mais combien d'occasions où l'on trouveroit de l'avantage à le substituer à la Peinture à l'huile plutôt que la détrempe. D'ailleurs, ceux qui ne sont pas bien habitués, pourroient, en s'exerçant quelquefois dans ce genre, acquérir de la prestesse & de la facilité, même du coloris. Nul doute au moins qu'il ne valut mieux, quand

on veut développer un sujet vaste, l'esquisser au pastel qu'à l'huile; cette manière prendroit peu de tems, seroit moins pénible, se prêteroit mieux aux corrections convenables, & seconderoit bien les élans & le feu de l'imagination.

10. Mais le pastel peut arracher beaucoup de jeunes personnes à l'ennui de la solitude. Ce genre de peinture a tant d'attraits, que rien n'est plus propre à leur fournir des ressources contre le désœuvrement, source de tant d'écarts. Le dessin fait partie de leur éducation. Mais elles s'y bornent, vu l'attirail qu'entraîne la Peinture. Cependant quel amusement plus doux, par exemple, ou qu'elle occupation plus délicieuse pour elles que de pouvoir tracer l'image des auteurs de leurs jours, des fleurs, un paysage. Le pastel leur en pré-

familiarizing themselves with this agreeable and easy kind of Painting.

8. No other approaches so much to nature. None produces such lifelike colours. Here is flesh, here is Flora, here is Aurora. If sometimes it has not so much force as oil Painting, this is less its own fault than that of the hand employing it.

9. Not that I wish to persuade anyone to give up the brush for pastel. But how many occasions when it would be to one's advantage to substitute pastel rather than tempera for oil Painting. Moreover, by trying their hand sometimes in this genre, those who are not fully conversant could acquire readiness and facility, even in colouring. No question at least that, when a large subject needs to be developed, it would be better to

sketch it out in pastel rather than oil. This manner would take little time, would be less toilsome, would lend itself better to suitable corrections, and would further the impulses and glow of the imagination.

10. But pastel can save many young people from the tedium of solitude. This kind of painting has so many attractions that nothing is better suited to offering them resources against idleness, the source of so many lapses. Drawing forms part of their education. But they limit themselves to that, in view of the equipment required by Painting. Yet what amusement more pleasant, for example, or what occupation more delightful for them than to be able to sketch out the likeness of their parents, or some flowers, or a landscape. Pastel offers them the readiest

fente les moyens les plus faciles. Ce n'eſt, pour ainſi dire, qu'un jeu.

11. Nous avons enfin pour objet de rendre aux Arts des talens découragés, en multipliant les reſſources & leur fourniſſant des moyens. La difficulté de deviner la préparation des crayons en paſtel, quoique bien ſimple quand on la connoît, rebute preſque tous ceux qui l'ignorent. Nous allons, dans cette vue, révéler ſans-doute plus d'un ſecret. Mais, dans les Beaux-Arts, le Génie ſeul doit en être un, parce qu'il ne peut ſe communiquer.

12. La compoſition méchanique des crayons en paſtel, ſera donc l'objet d'un des principaux articles de ce Traité.

CHAPITRE VI.

Des moyens de fixer le paſtel.

288. On conçoit bien que ſi l'on pouvoit faire pénêtrer dans la Peinture au paſtel quelque ſubſtance tranſparente & de nature concrète en diſſolution dans une liqueur, le paſtel reſteroit aſſujetti ſur le tableau dès que le paſtel auroit ſêché. Nul doute que ce ne fût un grand avantage, car la facilité de la Peinture au paſtel & la liberté qu'elle a de ſoigner, finir, retoucher un tableau tant qu'elle veut, lui donneroient bien des avantages ſur la freſque & ſur la détrempe. Mais comment appliquer une liqueur ſur des couleurs qui ſe détachent auſſitôt qu'on les touche.

means of doing so. It is, so to speak, a mere game.

11. Our object is lastly to bring disheartened talents back to the Arts, by multiplying its resources and providing them with means. The difficulty of divining the preparation of pastel crayons, though quite simple when known, rebuffs almost all those who are ignorant of it. In this survey we are doubtless going to reveal more than one secret. But in the Fine Arts it is Genius alone that need be one, because it cannot be communicated.

12. The mechanical composition of pastel crayons will therefore be dealt with in one of the main articles of this Treatise.

CHAPTER VI

On ways of fixing pastel

288. One may well imagine that if the pastel Painting could be permeated with some transparent substance, of a concrete nature when dissolved in a liquid, the pastel would remain fastened on the picture as soon as it had dried. No question but this would be a great advantage, for the easiness of pastel Painting and the freedom it affords for lingering over, finishing and retouching a picture as much as required, would give it many advantages over both fresco and tempera. But how to apply a liquid over colours that come away as soon as they are touched.

289. Cette difficulté se lève en un seul mot. Qu'on incorpore au pastel, au travers d'un tissu léger qui le garantisse du frottement, quelque liqueur propre à le pénétrer, de la matière solide & transparente dont elle sera chargée, & le voilà fixé.

Mais il ne faut pas juger sur cet apperçu du moyen que je propose. On va se convaincre qu'il est aussi sûr que simple, sur-tout si l'on se donne la peine d'en faire l'épreuve comme je vais l'expliquer.

290. D'abord le pastel ne s'enlève de dessus le canevas qu'autant qu'il éprouve quelque frottement ou qu'on le heurte avec un peu de violence.

Or, si l'on se contente de poser légèrement, sur la Peinture, un chassis monté d'un taffetas qui ne fasse qu'effleurer le pastel sans frot-

tement, ni secousse, il est clair qu'il n'en recevra pas la moindre altération, & que par conséquent l'on peut insinuer au travers de ce tissu la liqueur propre à fixer le pastel sans l'enlever ni l'effacer.

291. Cette principale difficulté levée, il ne s'agit que de trouver la substance convenable & la liqueur capable de s'en charger.

292. Parmi les matières concrètes & transparentes, les résines paroîtroient les substances les plus propres à cet usage ; de même qu'elles sont la base des vernis. Mais toutes, à l'exception du camphre, qui n'a point de consistance, changent entièrement la nuance des couleurs. On ne peut donc employer que les gommes ou les colles qui n'ont aucune couleur par elles-mêmes, lorsqu'elles ont peu

---

289. This difficulty may be removed with a single word. Let the pastel be blended, through a light fabric which shall secure it against rubbing, with some liquid capable of steeping it in the solid and transparent matter carried by that liquid, and the pastel will be fixed.

But the method I propose must not be judged from this summary of it. How sure and simple it is may be convincingly seen by taking the trouble of putting it to the test, as I shall now explain.

290. First of all, the pastel does not come off the canvas unless it undergoes some friction or is jostled with something of violence.

Now, if one will just fit the Painting lightly with a stretcher mounted with taffeta which shall just graze the pastel without friction or shaking, it is clear that it will not suffer the least alteration, and that consequently, through this fabric, one may introduce the liquid capable of fixing the pastel, without either removing it or effacing it.

291. This major difficulty being overcome, it only remains to find the right substance and the liquid capable of carrying it.

292. Among concrete and transparent substances, resins would appear to be the ones most suitable for this purpose, inasmuch as they are the basis for varnishes. But all of them, except for camphor, which has no consistence, entirely change the shade of the colours. So only gums and glues can be employed which

d'épaisseur, & qui n'altérent pas la nuance des matières colorées.

293. Mais comment les incorporer au pastel, si l'eau qui seule peut les dissoudre, ne peut, d'un autre côté, pénétrer certaines couleurs, telles que le bleu de Prusse, les laques? &c.

294. Voici la réponse. Il n'est aucune couleur dont l'esprit de vin ne pénêtre parfaitement la substance. Il est vrai qu'il ne peut dissoudre les gommes, non plus que l'eau ne peut dissoudre les résines. Mais si l'on combine ensemble l'une & l'autre liqueur, la difficulté s'évanouit. Il est évident qu'elles incorporeront au pastel la substance concrète dont elles sont chargées.

295. C'est en effet le résultat

qu'on obtiendra lorsqu'après avoir dissous dans l'eau quelque gomme ou colle, & versé dans cette eau partie à-peu-près égale d'esprit de vin, l'on humecte le pastel au travers d'un taffetas intermédiaire, avec un plumaceau chargé de ces deux liqueurs combinées. Le pastel sera sur le champ pénêtré par l'un & l'autre menstrue au travers du taffetas, qu'il faudra tout de suite enlever de dessus la Peinture aussi légèrement qu'on l'y a posé.

296. Peut-être pensera-t-on que le pastel doit alors s'attacher au tissu qui le touche. Il est vrai que j'en avois cette opinion moi-même au premier essai que j'en fis, & je fus étonné que le taffetas n'en eût rien enlevé quoique je n'eusse pas apporté de bien grandes précautions.

have no colour of their own, when they are thinned, and which do not alter the shade of the colouring matters.

293. But how to incorporate them into the pastel, if the water which alone can dissolve them, cannot on the other hand permeate certain colours, such as Prussian blue, lakes, etc.?

294. Here is the answer. There is no colour whose substance cannot be perfectly permeated by spirits of wine. It is true that it cannot dissolve the gums, just as water cannot dissolve the resins. But if the two liquids are combined together, the difficulty vanishes. It is evident that the two together will steep the pastel in the concrete substance with which they are charged.

295. This is the result that will be obtained when, after dissolving some gum or glue in water, and pouring into it about an equal part of spirits of wine, the pastel is moistened through an intervening taffeta with a feather-brush dipped in the two liquids combined. The pastel will at once be permeated by both solvents through the taffeta, which must be removed forthwith from over the Painting as lightly as it was laid there.

296. It may be thought that the pastel is likely to stick to the fabric touching it. It is true that I myself was of this opinion in the first trial that I made, and I was astonished to find that the taffeta had removed nothing of the pastel, even though I had taken no very great precautions.

The making of pastels is still today a craft technique, but its methods are undergoing continual development.

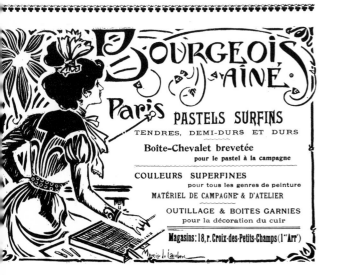

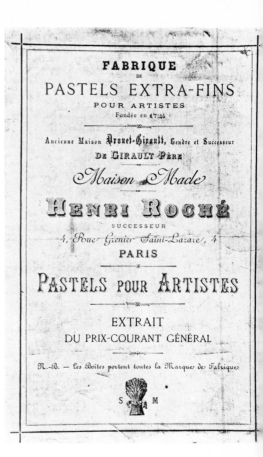

About 1875 the biologist and chemist Henri Roché founded in Paris the firm known today as La Maison du Pastel ("Pastel House"). He was prompted to do so by his meeting with a workman employed by an old art firm dating back to 1724, who acquainted him with the technical difficulties of making pastels. The workman, with his practical knowledge, and Roché, with his experimental mind and professional skills, sympathized and decided to join forces and manufacture their own pastels. Beginning with about a hundred shades, Roché soon extended the range to about five hundred, intent all the while on producing pastels of high quality, good adherence and easy handling. By 1914, after years of joint experiment with his son Dr Henri Roché, his catalogue could offer a thousand shades of colour. Since then the range has continued to widen and the firm today stocks something over 1650 different shades of pastel.

Owing to its ingredients the pastel stick is soft, fragile and crumbly. It should, however, be solid enough not to break when handled and not to crumble between the artist's fingers.

The pigments used in the making of pastel are identical with those used in the making of fine colours for artists, such as oil colours, watercolours, gouache, acrylic colours, and vinyl colours. From this it follows that the intrinsic qualities of pastel are similar to those of fine colours: stability in light and in mixtures.

The fact that pastel is light-fast and unfading is due entirely to the nature of the pigment; contrary to what some people think, no other ingredient has anything to do with it.

The manufacture of pastels depends on a sound balance between two extremes: hardness and softness. For in actual use both factors are important: the stick must be hard enough for easy handling, and soft enough for good adherence to the ground, which should be coarse-grained paper.

Harmonious balance between mechanical resistance and easy handling of the pastel is obtained by a very exact dosage of the raw materials entering into the make-up of pastel:

> pigments,
> mineral ingredients,
> gum-arabic solution.

Particular care must be taken in arriving at the right proportions, which depend on the nature of the pigment. At every stage of manufacture, these proportions may vary according to the qualities of the raw materials used.

The mineral ingredients constitute the physical base, while the pigments account for the more or less intense colouring of the substratum. Pigments and minerals are both employed in the form of a more or less fine powder.

The first phase of manufacture consists in weighing the different components, according to the basic formula.

The second phase is the grinding of pigments and minerals in the water binding them. The grinding is done with a grinding mill which consists of a loading funnel and two porcelain discs. The finely ground paste is more or less viscous; as it comes out of the grinding mill, it is caught in a linen cloth.

The third phase is the drying process. The paste is held in a strong piece of cloth, and the latter is folded over to form an envelope and passed through a press, squeezing out the water. This operation produces a "moist cake" which, after being crushed, is introduced into a stock and die.

The fourth phase, then, consists in introducing the hard paste into the stock and die and obtaining, from the pressure exerted upon it, a cylinder about one metre long.

This cylinder is placed upon a kind of wooden hurdle and while still soft is cut into the required lengths. After drying for about a fortnight, the pastel is ready for use.

Claude Curnier
Head of the Fine Arts Department
Firm of Lefranc & Bourgeois,
Paris, May 1983.

The secrets of the craft:
The pastel pigment, being dry and powdery and not easily adhering to the ground, has always raised practical problems for the artists using it. All of them have experimented with it and worked out their own formula for fixing the pigment to the chosen ground.

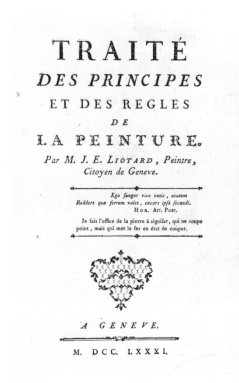

TRAITÉ
DES PRINCIPES
ET DES REGLES
DE
LA PEINTURE.

Par M. J. E. LIOTARD, Peintre,
Citoyen de Geneve.

Ego fungor vice cotis, acutum
Reddere quæ ferrum valet, excors ipsa secandi.
HOR. Art. Poet.

Je fais l'office de la pierre à aiguiser, qui ne coupe
point, mais qui met le fer en état de couper.

A GENEVE.

M. DCC. LXXXI.

Jean-Etienne Liotard:
"Treatise on the Principles
and Rules of Painting," title
page of the first edition,
Geneva, 1781.

Letter from Abbé Le Blanc to
Monsieur R.D.R. on the "Exhibition
of Works of Painting, Sculpture, etc.,"
Paris, 1747.

Several artists have been moved by jealousy to claim that Pastel is much easier to master than oil painting. This is far from being true of Pastel as we see it employed by La Tour. Such in any case is what I have heard said by many people of knowledge and experience who have seen him at work. The attempts made by some of those who would imitate him may fairly be called unsuccessful enough to make them change their opinion. In any endeavour it is easy to go on in the common way; the difficult thing is to excel. I have no hesitation in saying that the Pastel Portraits of La Tour have one considerable advantage over those painted in oils, and that is that they will not change. Oil darkens with time and dims the brightness of the finest colours. How many Pictures of the greatest Masters are now so altered that one cannot make out anything in them? Pastel covered with a glazing defies the ravages of air; it is unchanging. Pastel moreover is more lifelike for Portraiture. Oil has a sheen and gloss that are not in nature, which is rendered much more faithfully by the lustreless tone of Pastel. La Tour, as I have said, has overcome the only difficulty connected with it. Pastel failed to last, because those who had used it hitherto did not know how to make it adhere. Many of the fine things by *Rosa Alba* have already perished. The varnish used by La Tour, of which I have said something, fixes his works without taking off their bloom. This colouring, so strong and true, which he has given to all his Portraits will always be the same. His works will last as long as it is given to human things to last.

"The Salon" by Jacques La Combe,
Paris, 1753.

You have often complained, Sir, that for Portraits people were giving the preference to Pastel over Pictures painted in oils. And, indeed, Pastel always has a crudeness, a mealy dustiness, a hard and disagreeable touch to it, that Art and talent cannot entirely retrieve. It is true that the glaze gives it a bright varnish. But that glaze disguises its shortcomings without remedying them; moreover it does not prevent the grain of the pastel stick from subsequently falling away and the bloom of the Painting from disappearing little by little. La Tour it is who has doubtless

contributed most to establishing this dominant fashion. The soul that breathes within his Pastels has carried all before it. This famous Artist has exhibited at the Salon several of these masterpieces of Art which one cannot weary of admiring.

Proceedings of the Academy,
Paris, 1764.

A report has been made to the Academy by Professor Hallé, Assistant Professor Bachelier, Counsellor de La Tour and Academician Roslin, to the effect that in several trials they have used and tested a new way of priming with oils the canvas or taffeta to which the pastels are applied. The result is that the pastel adheres to it and takes on all the consistency of an oil painting; that they have found it easy and cheap to use; and that the various trials made with the pictures painted in this fashion have caused no alteration in them. Consequently, at the request of Dame Pellechet, widow of the late Mr Pellechet, who invented this new preparation, the Academy hereby declares that it considers this discovery as being highly useful for the practice of the Arts, and one that deserves to be encouraged.

Letter from Maurice Quentin de La Tour
to Isabelle van Zuylen (later
Madame de Charrière), 1770.

I would have advised you not to overwork the colours when they are right, to use your little finger as lightly as possible, not to employ too much colour and to keep the paper untouched where you wish to apply a heavy layer of chalk; in this way the work will be much more lightly done.
As for the mould resulting from the salt content of black chalk and of nearly all pastels, it must be prevented from coalescing, thickening; by simply rubbing it on the paper, a stain can be avoided. You then remove it with the point of a knife; but you should first hold a hot iron close to it, to dry up the moist salt and facilitate removal with the knife. This is the process I have been using lately. I have also been treating blue paper with a light wash, applied with a brush, of yellow ochre diluted with water and egg-yolk; this obviates the heaviness which it is difficult to avoid when using the quantity of colours needed to cover the blue of the paper.

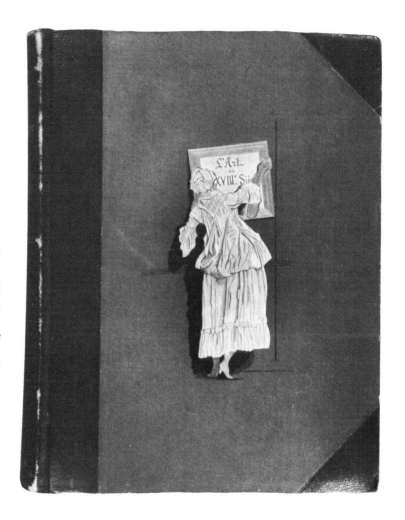

Edmond and Jules de Goncourt,
L'Art du XVIIIe siècle,
Paris, 1882.

All his life La Tour experimented with the varnish fixative. Abbé Le Blanc, in his *Lettre sur l'exposition des ouvrages de peinture* of 1747, says that "the varnish used by La Tour fixes his works without taking off their bloom, and that his works will last as long as it is given to human things to last." That same year, in his *Réflexions nouvelles d'un amateur*, Lieudé de Septmanville says: "It is true that La Tour went to endless pains to find out a varnish which in fact was a complete failure and totally ruined a large number of his pictures. He is known to have offered a sum of money to Mr Charmeton, who had flattered himself with having found out the way to make pastel adhere. It is admitted that he discovered by his own pains a *subtle body* of some kind with which he claimed that he was able to give more consistency to this way of painting." This fixative was in fact being sought for throughout the eighteenth century. The fashion for pastel was then such that "it put coloured crayons in the hands of everyone," in the hands of men and women, of the Chevalier de Boufflers and Madame de Charrière, and peopled the Place Dauphine exhibitions with the pastels of the Montjoies, who were pupils of La Tour. They all vied with each other in devising procedures and secrets to make these fragile paintings last a little longer. From 1758 to 1773 the *Avant-Coureur* kept announcing one discovery after another. The Demoiselles Beauvais advised the public that they had found a secret for fixing pastel without altering the beauty and vivacity of the colours. A Sieur Mauge, in a long letter, told the public all about a new procedure. A Sieur Bréa stated that you could run your hand, and even a pumice stone, over the pastels fixed by his method. Monsieur de Saint-Michel, a Piedmontese gentleman, painter to the King of Sardinia, and holding a certificate from Cochin, boasted of having contrived to fix pastels in an unalterable manner and having found the ingredients for a very fine pastel stick; he proposed his secret to a thousand subscribers, at sixty gold francs apiece, for which they would each receive a book containing his famous recipes. An account was given of the method used by the Prince of San Severo, based on fish glue. Another fixative was described: it consisted in covering the whole pastel with the dust of gum arabic passed through a strainer, dissolving this dust with hot steam and then coating the pastel with oil varnish. Monsieur de Monpetit attacked all these methods, which he charged with darkening and overloading the pastel tones, and singled out the invention of Loriot, which he regarded as the best. Loriot's secret was finally divulged and published in 1780 by Renou, secretary of the Royal Academy of Painting. As for La Tour's secret, whose effect can be studied at Saint-Quentin, it is still locked up in an autograph letter by the painter, which Monsieur Villot was expected to publish.

A famous example of unremitting experimentation is provided by Degas, and analysed by Denis Rouart in his writings on the painter.

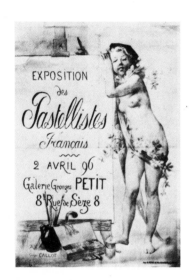

That pastel was used by artists fairly often to correct their oil paintings, seems likely enough. But this amounts to no more than temporary retouchings, laid in with a view to judging of the rightness or wrongness of certain modifications before carrying them out finally and irremediably in oils. The nature of such work is therefore essentially different from the mixed media studied in the previous pages.

Degas's true invention undoubtedly lay in this application of successive coats of pastel, each one of them being fixed before it was overlaid with the next. He contrived to adapt pastels to this technique which consists in making play with different colours among themselves by superposition and transparency as much as by the opposition of juxtaposed tones. This transparency cannot be obtained by the actual paint-

Poster by Georges Callot for an exhibition of French pastellists, Georges Petit Gallery, Paris, 1896.

Pavilion of the Pastel and Watercolour Painters, Paris World's Fair, 1889.

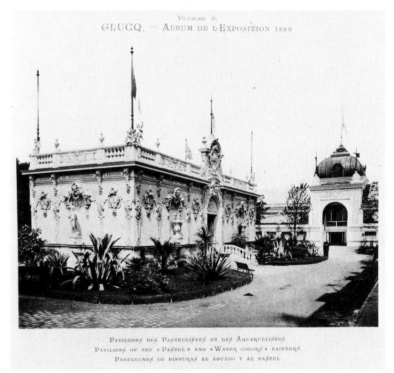

In his attempts to vary the picture texture, Degas also hit upon an original procedure. After laying in his subject with pastels, he blew hot steam over that sketch. He thus reduced this colour dust to the condition of a paste, which he then worked over with a more or less hard brush. Or again, if the boiling water was vaporized over fairly thin pastel, instead of a paste he obtained a wash which he spread with the brush. He naturally refrained from projecting the water vapour over every part of his picture, leaving the original pastel untouched in certain places. This gave him a different handling for the various elements making up his picture. A dancer's flesh was not treated in the same way as her skirt, and the texture of the setting was different from that of the floor. So the result was analogous to those obtained by the methods previously described, and always ended in a mixture of brushwork and pastel crayon.

Both in his way of moistening the pastel and in his habit of varying the execution by introducing another technique of painting such as tempera or gouache, Degas seems indeed to have been the first to combine the brushwork with the work of the coloured crayon.

In the years 1892-1895 Degas would sketch out his picture with colours already very rich and forthright, and this initial coating would be firmly fixed. Then he would work over the coloured surface thus obtained without any fear that his crayons might impair the tones already laid in. Allowing the undercoat to show through here and there, he would set the new colours playing over this ground, thus neutralizing some and reinforcing others. This operation of fixing and applying colours would be repeated several times until the picture was completed; until, that is, he had brought it to the point where he felt satisfied with the work—a point which, as is well known, was arrived at with difficulty.

work of pastel, as it can by oil paints glazed over. So that he had to arrive at an analogous effect, by not entirely covering the picture surface and leaving unpainted areas where the underpainting could show through.

The great difficulty of this procedure lay in taking care not to damage the previous coat over which he had to work. To protect it required a fixative of the best kind, and after trying out a lot of them Degas was much helped in his search by Luigi Chialiva. The idea of this method, however, was entirely his own.

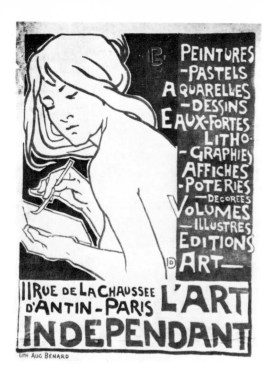

Poster by Auguste Bénard
for an exhibition of
"Independent Art," Paris,
1897.

Catalogue cover for the exhibition
"Papers from Nature," organized by
Jean Clair and Dominique Pallut at
the Autumn Festival, Paris, 1977.

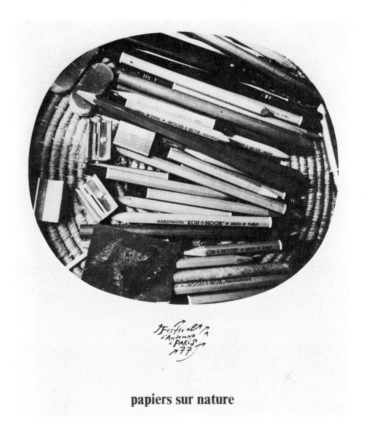

papiers sur nature

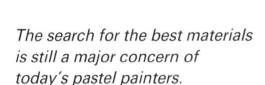

*The search for the best materials
is still a major concern of
today's pastel painters.*

Curiously enough, the marketing of excellent fixatives has not changed the pastel technique. Yet the fixative could be to pastel what oil is to oil paints—a medium. (Just think of Degas and his obsession with a fixative that would allow him to work in terms of transparency.)

The eighteenth-century pastel, essentially a portrait pastel elaborated on the spot, was not called upon to travel. Today the contrary is true of every work that is meant to be exhibited. Being subject to the risks of travel, it has to be fixed and well fixed, or it will go to pieces. And the fixative can not only cut down the tone by half but almost overwhelm it or reduce it to a gouache, which must be avoided at any cost.

Since pastel owes its quality to the graininess by which the light is refracted, it is very difficult to achieve transparencies while preserving its "bloom." It is a matter of fixing sand on sand, fixing at every moment in order to prevent each new coat from tearing away or dimming the undercoat, in order to obtain in the end that porous, sonorous and luminous paintwork incomparable in its éclat.

From the heightened drawing it was at the start, pastel may claim to become a full-fledged painting in the hands of a bold artist capable of judiciously employing a good fixative, the colours remaining pure, unlike those of oil painting which are seriously and unavoidably altered as the picture ages.

François Barbâtre, February 1983

121

Bibliography

List of illustrations

Index of names
and places

Bibliography

General Works

ANONYMOUS, *Secrets concernant les arts et métiers...*, 2 vols., Brussels, 1747. – ANONYMOUS (M.P.R. de C.), *Traité de la peinture au pastel*, Paris, 1788.

F. BALDINUCCI, *Notizie dei Professori del disegno da Cimabue in qua*, Florence, 1681-1728; reprint, 7 vols., Florence, 1974-1975. – C. BAZIN, *Petit traité ou Méthode de peinture. Pastel*, Paris, 1849. – R. BRETEAU, *Pastels*, Paris, 1946. – L. BRIEGER, *Das Pastell, seine Geschichte und seine Meister*, Berlin, 1921.

G. CASTER, *Le commerce du pastel et de l'épicerie à Toulouse de 1450 environ à 1561*, Toulouse, 1962. – *Catalogus van de tentoongestelde schilderijen pastels en aquarellen*, Rijksmuseum, Amsterdam, 1951 and 1956. – *Catalogue: Besançon, le plus ancien Musée de France*, Musée des Arts Décoratifs, Paris, 1957. – *Catalogue des pastels, gouaches, miniatures*, Musée des Beaux-Arts, Dijon, 1972.

O. FIDIÈRE, *Les femmes artistes à l'Académie Royale de peinture et de sculpture*, Paris, 1885. – A. FONTAINE, *Les collections de l'Académie Royale de Peinture*, Paris, 1930.

H. GAUTIER DE NISMES, *L'art de laver...*, Paris, 1687. – F. GOUPIL, *Le pastel simplifié et perfectionné. Etude expérimentale d'après les méthodes comparées des meilleurs maîtres*, Paris, n.d. (new edition, 1949); *Pastel Painting simplified and perfected...*, Philadelphia, 1886; *Initiation au pastel*, Paris, 1976. – D. E. GREENE, *Pastel*, New York-London, 1974. – P. GREGORIUS, *Syntaxeon Artis Mirabilis*, Cologne, 1583.

R. HAHN, *Pastellmalerei, eine Einführung in die Technik*, Ravensburg, 1940. – P. HATTIS, *Four Centuries of French Drawings in the Fine Arts Museum of San Francisco*, San Francisco, 1977.

P. JAMOT, *La peinture en France*, Paris, 1934. – JOMBERT, *Méthode pour apprendre le dessin*, Paris, 1755.

W. KOSCHATZKY, K. OBERHUBER, E. KNAB, *I grandi disegni italiani dell'Albertina di Vienna*, Milan, 1971.

G. de LAIRESSE, *Les principes du dessein*, Amsterdam, 1719. – P. LA-VALLÉE, *Le dessin français du XIIIe au XVIe siècle*, Paris, 1930; *Les techniques du dessin. Leur évolution dans les différentes écoles de l'Europe*, Paris, 1943, 1949.

M. MATOSÈS, Mme MATOSÈS-DUMAS, P. MATOSÈS, *Cours de dessin. Aquarelle, peinture, pastel, gouache, miniature*, Angoulême, 1934. – J. MEDER, *Die Handzeichnung. Ihre Technik und Entwicklung*, Vienna, 1919, 1923. – G. MONNIER, *Musée du Louvre, Cabinet des Dessins. Petits guides des grands musées. Le pastel*, Pavillon de Flore, Paris, 1979.

L. NORMAN, A. MOGELON, B. THOMPSON, *Pastel, Charcoal and Chalk Drawing: History, Classical and Contemporary Techniques*, London, 1973.

W. OSTWALD, *Monumentales und dekoratives Pastell*, Leipzig, 1912.

R. de PILES, *Les premiers éléments de la peinture pratique*, Paris, 1684.

L. RICHMOND, *The Art of Painting in Pastel*, introduction by Frank Brangwyn, London, 1917; *The Technique of Pastel Painting*, London, 1931. – J. RIGAUD, *Renseignements sur les Beaux-Arts à Genève*, Geneva, 1876. – J. ROBERT, *Nouvelle méthode à la portée de tous. Le pastel*, Paris, 1908; *Le Pastel*, Paris, 1933. – K. ROBERT, *Le Pastel*, Paris, 1884 (new edition, 1950). – J. RUSSELL, *Elements of Painting with Crayons*, London, 1772.

E. L. SEARS, *Pastel Painting Step by Step*, New York, 1968.

J. P. THENOT, *Le pastel appris sans maître, ou l'Art chez soi*, edited by F. GOUPIL, Paris, 1881 (new edition, 1948).

FROM THE 16th TO THE 18th CENTURY

General Works and Monographs

V. L. ADAIR, *Eighteenth Century Pastel Portraits*, London, 1971. – J. ADHÉMAR, *Le dessin français au XVIᵉ siècle*, Lausanne, 1954. – A. ANANOFF, *L'œuvre dessiné de F. Boucher, Catalogue raisonné*, Paris, 1966.

O. BENESCH, *Master Drawings in the Albertina. European Drawings from the 15th to the 18th Century*, New York, 1967. – A. BESNARD and G. WILDENSTEIN, *La Tour, La vie et l'œuvre de l'artiste, Catalogue raisonné*, Paris, 1928. – H. BOUCHOT, *Portraits au crayon*, Paris, 1884. – J. BOUCHOT-SAUPIQUE, *Musée National du Louvre, Catalogue des pastels*, Paris, 1930. – A. BURY, *La Tour*, London, 1971.

R. CARRIERA, *Diario degli anni 1720 e 1721 scritto di propria mano in Parigia...*, Venice, 1793; French edition, *Journal de Rosalba Carriera pendant son séjour à Paris en 1720 et 1721*, edited by Alfred Sensier, Paris, 1865. – F. CESSI, *Rosalba Carriera*, Milan, 1965. – A. DOBSON, *Rosalba's Journal and Other Papers*, London, 1915.

E. DACIER and P. RATOUIS de LIMAY, *Pastels français du XVIIᵉ et XVIIIᵉ siècle*, Paris-Brussels, 1927. – A. DAYOT and J. GUIFFREY, *J. B. Siméon Chardin*, Paris, n.d. – A. DAYOT and L. VAILLAT, *L'œuvre de J. B. S. Chardin et de J. H. Fragonard*, Paris, 1907. – A. N. DÉZALLIER d'ARGENVILLE, *Abrégé de la vie des plus fameux peintres*, Paris, 1762. – Lady DILKE, *French Painters of the Eighteenth Century*, London, 1899. – L. DIMIER, *Les Clouet*, 1924; *Histoire de la peinture de portrait en France au XVIᵉ siècle*, 3 vols., Paris-Brussels, 1928-1930. – E. DRÉOLLE de NODON, *Eloge biographique de Maurice Quentin La Tour*, Paris, 1856. – Abbé DUPLAQUET, *Eloge historique de M. Maurice Quentin La Tour*, Saint-Quentin, 1789.

E. FLEURY and G. BRIÈRE, *Catalogue des pastels de M. Q. de La Tour. Collections à Saint-Quentin et Musée du Louvre*, Paris, 1920; *Collections à Saint-Quentin*, 1932 (reprint, 1954). – M. FLORISOONE, *Portraits français*, Paris, 1946; *Le XVIIIᵉ siècle*, Paris, 1948. – F. FOSCA, *La vie, les voyages et les œuvres de Jean-Etienne Liotard*, Lausanne-Paris, 1956. – I. de FOURCAUD, *J. B. Siméon Chardin*, Paris, 1900.

K. GARLICK, *Introduction to the Catalogue of the Paintings, Drawings and Pastels of T. Lawrence*, Glasgow, 1964. – E. de GONCOURT, *Catalogue raisonné de l'Œuvre peint, dessiné et gravé de P. P. Prud'hon*, Paris, 1876; *La Maison d'un artiste*, Paris, 1881. – E. and J. de GONCOURT, *L'Art au XVIIIᵉ siècle*, 2 vols., Paris, 1859-1875; *Madame de Pompadour*, Paris, 1878. – J. GUIFFREY, *Table générale des artistes ayant exposé aux Salons du XVIIIᵉ siècle*, 1873; *Catalogue de l'œuvre de J. B. S. Chardin*, Paris, 1908; *Musée du Louvre. P. P. Prud'hon, peintures, pastels et dessins*, Paris, 1924; *L'œuvre de P. P. Prud'hon*, Paris, 1924. – J. GUIFFREY and P. MARCEL, *Inventaire général des dessins du Musée du Louvre et du Musée de Versailles. Ecole française*, 10 vols., Paris, 1907-1928.

G. HENRIOT, *Collection David Weill*, 5 vols., Paris, 1926-1929. – L. HAUTECŒUR, "Liotard portraitiste de la famille impériale" in *Musées de Genève*, October 1947.

T. D. KAMENSKAYA, *Pasteli Khudoznikov zapadnoevropeiskikh skola XVI-XIX vekov*, Leningrad, 1960. – T. KLINGSOR, *Chardin*, Paris, 1924.

H. LAPAUZE, *La Tour, son œuvre au musée de Saint-Quentin*, Paris, 1905. – P. LAVALLÉE, *Dessins français du XVIIIᵉ siècle à la Bibliothèque de l'Ecole des Beaux-Arts*, Paris, 1928. – A. LEROY, *Quentin de La Tour et la Société française du XVIIIᵉ siècle*, Paris, 1953. – P. de LESPINASSE, *La miniature en France au XVIIIᵉ siècle*, Paris-Brussels, 1929. – O. LEVERTIN, *G. Lundberg*, Stockholm, 1902. – G. W. LUNDBERG, *Madame Roslin*, Malmö, 1934. – R. LOCHE, *Jean-Etienne Liotard*, Geneva, 1976. – R. LOCHE and M. ROTHLISBERGER, *L'opera completa del Liotard*, Milan, 1978. – J. J. LUMA, "Dos retratos al pastel de Vivien" in *Archivo español de Arte*, 1977.

H. MACFALL, *The French Pastellists of the 18th Century*, London, 1909. – C. MAGNIER, *Madame de Pompadour et La Tour*, Saint-Quentin, 1904. – D. MAHON, *Studies in Seicento Art and Theory*, London, 1947. – V. MALAMANI, *Rosalba Carriera*, Bergamo, 1910. – P. MANTZ, *François Boucher, Lemoyne et Natoire*, Paris, 1880. – A. MICHEL, *François Boucher*, Paris, 1907. – G. MONNIER, *Inventaire des collections publiques françaises. Musée du Louvre. Cabinet des dessins, Pastels XVIIᵉ et XVIIIᵉ siècles*, Paris, 1972; "Expositions, Musée du Louvre, Cabinet des dessins, Pastels et miniatures du XVIIIᵉ siècle", in *Revue du Louvre et des Musées de France*, Vol. 23, Paris, 1973.

P. de NOLHAC, *Madame Vigée-Lebrun, peintre de la Reine Marie-Antoinette*, Paris, 1908; *Boucher, Premier peintre du Roi*, Paris, 1925; *La vie et l'œuvre de Maurice Quentin de La Tour*, Paris, 1930; *Portraits du XVIIIᵉ siècle*, Paris, 1933.

H. OLSEN, *Federico Barocci*, Copenhagen, 1962. – C. OULMONT, *Les Femmes peintres au XVIIIᵉ siècle*, Paris, 1928.

R. PALLUCCHINI, *La pittura veneziana del Settecento*, Venice-Rome, 1960. – A. M. PASSEZ, *A. Labille-Guiard (1749-1803). Biographie et Catalogue raisonné de son œuvre*, Paris, 1973. – C. de PELOUX, *Répertoire biographique et bibliographique des artistes du XVIIIᵉ siècle français*, Paris, 1930. – R. PORTALIS, *Adelaïde Labille-Guiard*, Paris, 1902. – G. PREVITALI, *Jean-Etienne Liotard*, Milan, 1966.

P. RATOUIS de LIMAY, *Musée du Louvre, Les pastels du XVIIᵉ et XVIIIᵉ siècle*, Paris, 1925; *Le pastel en France au XVIIIᵉ siècle*, Paris, 1946. – L. RÉAU, *Histoire de la peinture française au XVIIIᵉ siècle*, Paris-Brussels, 1925; *L'Art au XVIIIᵉ siècle, époque Louis XVI*, Paris, 1952. – L. ROGER-MILES, *Maîtres du XVIIIᵉ siècle. Cent pastels*, Paris, 1908. – P. ROSENBERG, *Chardin*, Geneva-New York, 1963.

A. SCHÖNBERGER and H. SOEHNER, *The Rococo Age. Art and Civilization of the 18th Century*, New York and London, 1960. – R. M. SEE, *English Pastels*, London, 1911. – J. SEZNEC and J. ADHÉMAR, *Diderot, Salons*, 4 vols., Oxford, 1957-1967. – D. SUTTON, *French Drawings of the 18th Century*, London, 1949.

C. de TOLNAY, *History and Technique of Old Master Drawings*, New York, 1943. – M. TOURNEUX, *La Tour*, Paris, 1904. – N. S. TRIVAS, "Les natures mortes de Liotard" in *Gazette des Beaux-Arts*, I, 1936; "Les portraits de J. E. Liotard par lui-même" in *Revue de l'art ancien et moderne*, 1936.

L. VAILLAT and P. RATOUIS de LIMAY, *J. B. Perronneau*, Paris, 1909 (new edition, 1923). – F. VALCANOVER, *Chardin*, Paris, 1967. – A. WALTHER, *Zu den Werken der Rosalba Carriera in der Dresdener Gemäldegalerie*, Dresden, 1972-1975. – D. WILDENSTEIN, *Inventaires après décès d'artistes et de collectionneurs français du XVIIIe siècle*, Paris, 1967. – G. WILDENSTEIN, *Chardin*, Paris, 1933, 1963. – G. C. WILLIAMSON, *John Russell, R. A.*, London, 1894.

Exhibitions

1886: *Jean-Etienne Liotard*, Société des Arts, Geneva. – **1907**: *Drawings and Gouaches principally of the 18th Century*, Colony Club, New York. – **1908**: *Cent pastels au XVIIIe siècle*, Galerie Georges Petit, Paris. – **1911**: *Pastellistes anglais au XVIIIe siècle*, Galerie Brunner, Paris; *La Turquerie et la Chinoiserie au XVIIIe siècle*, Musée des Arts Décoratifs, Paris. – **1925**: *Jean-Etienne Liotard*, Musée d'Art et d'Histoire, Geneva. – **1933**: *Pastels français du XVIIe siècle à nos jours*, Galerie Seligmann, Paris. – **1945**: *Les Artistes suédois en France au XVIIIe siècle*, Château de Versailles. – **1948**: *Liotard et Füssli*, Musée d'Art et d'Histoire, Geneva. – **1949**: *Pastels des collections nationales et du Musée La Tour de Saint-Quentin*, Orangerie des Tuileries, Paris. – **1955**: *De David à Toulouse-Lautrec*, Orangerie des Tuileries, Paris. – **1957-1958**: *Le portrait français de Watteau à David*, Orangerie des Tuileries, Paris. – **1958**: *Zeitalter des Rokoko, Kunst und Kultur im 18. Jahrhundert*, Munich. – **1959**: *Disegni fiorentini del Museo del Louvre della collezione di F. Baldinucci*, Farnesina alla Lungara, Rome. – **1964**: *Le dessin français dans les collections hollandaises*, Paris-Amsterdam. – **1967**: *Le Cabinet d'un grand amateur P. J. Mariette*, Musée du Louvre, Paris. – **1968**: *France in the 18th Century*, Royal Academy, London. – **1969**: *Dal Ricci al Tiepolo. I pittori di figura del Settecento a Venezia*, Palazzo Ducale, Venice; *Dessins français du XVIIIe siècle*, Galerie de l'Œil, Paris. – **1970**: *Les Clouet et la cour des rois de France. De François Ier à Henri IV*, Bibliothèque Nationale, Paris. – **1975**: *Dessins italiens de l'Albertina de Vienne*, Cabinet des Dessins, Louvre, Paris; *Federico Barocci*, Museo Civico, Bologna; *Eloge de l'ovale: peintures et pastels du XVIIIe siècle français*, Galerie Cailleux, Paris. – **1976-1977**: *Dessins français de l'Art Institute of Chicago. De Watteau à Picasso*, Cabinet des Dessins, Louvre, Paris; *Woman Artists 1550-1960*, Los Angeles County Museum of Art. – **1978**: *Jean-Etienne Liotard*, Kunsthaus, Zürich. – **1979**: *Chardin*, Grand Palais, Paris. – **1980**: *Portrait et Société en France (1715-1789)*, Palais de Tokyo, Paris; *The Painterly Print. Monotypes from the Seventeenth to the Twentieth Century*, Metropolitan Museum of Art, New York. – **1981-1982**: *Dessins baroques florentins du Musée du Louvre*, Cabinet des Dessins, Louvre, Paris. – **1982**: *Le Portrait en Italie au siècle de Tiepolo*, Petit Palais, Paris.

19th CENTURY

General Works and Monographs

H. ADHÉMAR and A. DAYEZ, *Musée du Jeu de Paume*, Paris, 1973. – H. ADHÉMAR, M. BEAULIEU, M. OLIVIER, G. MONNIER, *Degas. Œuvres du Musée du Louvre*, Paris, 1969. – J. ADHÉMAR and F. CACHIN, *Degas, gravures et monotypes*, Paris, 1973. – J. ALBOIZE, "Les pastellistes français" in *L'Artiste*, April 1889. – F. ARCANGELI and M. C. GOZZOLI, *L'opera completa di Segantini*, Milan, 1973.

R. BACOU, *Millet, Dessins*, Paris, 1975; *Odilon Redon*, Geneva, 1956. – M. L. BATAILLE and G. WILDENSTEIN, *Berthe Morisot. Catalogue des peintures, pastels et aquarelles*, Paris, 1961. – K. BERGER, *Französische Meister-Zeichnungen des 19. Jahrhunderts*, Basel, 1949; *Odilon Redon: Fantasy and Colour*, New York, 1965. – R. J. BOYLE, *American Impressionism*, Boston, 1974. – A. D. BREESKIN, *Mary Cassatt. A Catalogue Raisonné of the Oils, Pastels, Watercolors and Drawings*, Washington, 1970. – R. BRETTELL and C. LLOYD, *Catalogue of the Drawings by Camille Pissarro in the Ashmolean Museum*, Oxford, 1980. – E. J. BULLARD, *Mary Cassatt: Oils and Pastels*, New York, 1972.

G. CAPRONI and G. M. SUGANA, *Tutta l'opera di Toulouse-Lautrec*, Milan, 1977. – *Catalogue: Albi, Musée Toulouse-Lautrec*, Palais de la Barbie, Albi, 1967. – *Catalogue: Paris, Musée du Jeu de Paume*, Paris, 1973. – J. CHIALIVA, "Comment Degas a changé sa technique du dessin" in *Bulletin de la Société de l'Histoire de l'Art français*, Paris, 1932. – D. COOPER, *Zeichnungen und Aquarelle von Vincent van Gogh*, Basel, 1954; *Pastels by Edgar Degas*, New York, 1953. – J. CASSOU, *Odilon Redon*, Antwerp, 1974.

F. DAULTE, *Pierre-Auguste Renoir, Aquarelles, pastels et dessins en couleurs*, Basel, 1958. – R. L. DELEVOY, de CROES, C. OLLINGER, G. ZINQUE, *Fernand Khnopff et Catalogue de l'œuvre*, Brussels, 1979. – M. G. DORTU, *Toulouse-Lautrec et son œuvre*, 6 vols., Paris, 1971. – I. H. E. DUNLOP, *Degas*, London, 1979. – B. DUNSTAN, "The Pastel Techniques of Edgar Degas" in *American Artist*, September 1972.

A. FERMIGIER, *Millet*, Geneva-New York, 1977. – C. FLERS, "Du Pastel. De son application au paysage en particulier" in *L'Artiste*, Paris, 1846. – P. FRANCASTEL, *Monet, Sisley, Pissarro*, Paris, 1939.

P. GEORGEL and L. ROSSI BARTOLOTTO, *Tout l'œuvre peint de Delacroix*, Paris, 1975.

L. HAUTECŒUR and P. LADOUÉ, *Musée du Luxembourg. Catalogue des peintures et sculptures*, Paris, 1933. – R. L. HERBERT, "Millet revisited" in *Burlington Magazine*, July 1962; "Millet reconsidered" in *Museum Studies*, Chicago, I, 1966. – R. HOBBS, *Odilon Redon*, Boston, 1977. – P. HUISMAN and M. G. DORTU, *Lautrec par Lautrec*, Paris, 1964.

G. JEAN-AUBRY, *Eugène Boudin. La vie, l'œuvre d'après les lettres et documents inédits*, Neuchâtel, 1968. – M. JOYANT, *Henri de Toulouse-Lautrec*, 2 vols., Paris, 1926-1927. – E. JULIEN, *Lautrec*, Paris, n.d. – P. JULLIAN, *Les Symbolistes*, Neuchâtel, 1973.

G. de KNYFF, *Eugène Boudin raconté par lui-même*, Paris, 1976.

J. B. de LA FAILLE, *L'œuvre de Vincent Van Gogh*, Paris-Brussels, 1928. – J. LASSAIGNE and F. MINERVINO, *Tout l'œuvre peint de Degas*, Paris, 1974. – F. C. LEGRAND, *Le Symbolisme en Belgique*, Brussels, 1971. – P. A. LEMOISNE, *Degas et son œuvre*, 4 vols., Paris, 1947-1949. – J. LEYMARIE, *Les Degas du Louvre*, Paris, 1947; *Paul Gauguin, Aquarelles, pastels et dessins*, Basel, 1960. – C. LLOYD, *Camille Pissarro*, Geneva-London-New York, 1981.

M. MALINGUE, *Gauguin, le peintre et son œuvre*, Paris-London, 1948. – K. MARTIN, *Edouard Manet, Aquarelles et pastels*, Basel, 1958. – J. MEIER-GRAEFE, *Renoir*, Leipzig, 1929. – T. F. MESSER, *Edvard Munch*, New York, 1973. – A. MOEN, *Edvard Munch*, 3 vols., Oslo, 1957-1958. – E. MOREAU-NÉLATON, *Delacroix raconté par lui-même*, 2 vols., Paris, 1916; *Millet raconté par lui-même*, 3 vols., Paris, 1921; *Manet raconté par lui-même*, Paris, 1926.

Bibliography

T. NATANSON, *Peints à leur tour*, Paris, 1948.

E. PARRY-JANIS, ''The Role of the Monotype in the Working Method of Degas'' in *Burlington Magazine*, 1967; *Degas Monotypes*, Cambridge, Mass., 1968. – L. R. PISSARRO and L. VENTURI, *Camille Pissaro, son art, son œuvre*, Paris, 1939.

O. REDON, *A Soi-même. Journal (1867-1915)*, Paris, 1922. – T. REFF, *Degas, The Artist's Mind*, New York, 1976. – J. D. REY, *Berthe Morisot*, Paris, 1982. – J. REWALD, *Renoir Drawings*, New York, 1946; *The History of Impressionism*, New York, 1946, 1961, 1973; *Edouard Manet, Pastels*, Oxford, 1947; *Post-Impressionism, From Van Gogh to Gauguin*, New York, 1956; *Gauguin Drawings*, New York, 1958. – A. de RIDDER, *William Degouve de Nuncques*, Brussels, 1957. – K. ROBERTS, *Degas*, Oxford, 1976 (new edition, 1982). – M. ROSKILL, *Van Gogh, Gauguin and the Impressionist Circle*, Greenwich, Conn., 1970. – D. ROUART, *Degas à la recherche de sa technique*, Paris, 1945; ''Degas, paysages en monotype'' in *L'Œil*, September 1964, No. 117. – D. ROUART and S. ORIENTI, *Tout l'œuvre peint de Manet*, Paris, 1970. – D. ROUART and D. WILDENSTEIN, *Edouard Manet. Catalogue raisonné, Peintures*, 3 vols., Lausanne, 1974-1979.

S. SANDSTROM, *Le monde imaginaire d'Odilon Redon*, Lund, 1955. – M. SCHAPIRO, *Van Gogh*, New York, 1950. – G. SCHIEFFLER, *Edvard Munch. Graphische Kunst*, Dresden, 1923; *Edvard Munch. Das graphische Werk (1906-1926)*, Berlin, 1928. – R. SCHMIT, *Eugène Boudin (1824-1898)*, 3 vols., Paris, 1973. – J. SELZ, *Odilon Redon*, Paris, 1971. – A. SENSIER and P. MANTZ, *La vie et l'œuvre de J. F. Millet*, Paris, 1881. – P. SÉRUSIER, *ABC de la peinture*, Paris, 1921. – C. STERLING and H. ADHÉMAR, *Musée du Louvre. Peintures. Ecole Française, XIXᵉ siècle*, 4 vols., Paris, 1958-1961. – J. SUTHERLAND-BOGGS, *Portraits by Degas*, Berkeley-Los Angeles, 1962. – D. SUTTON, *Lautrec*, London, 1962; *Whistler, Paintings, Etchings, Pastels and Watercolours*, London, 1966.

A. TABARANT, *Manet. Histoire catalographique.* Paris, 1931; *Manet et ses œuvres*, Paris, 1947.

L. VENTURI, *Les archives de l'impressionnisme*, 2 vols., Paris, 1939. – A. VOLLARD, ''Degas et la technique'' in *Beaux-Arts*, No. 219, 1937; *Renoir, An Intimate Portrait*, New York, 1925; *Degas, An Intimate Portrait*, New York, 1927; *Souvenirs d'un marchand de tableaux*, Paris, 1948.

A. WERNER, *Degas, Pastels*, New York, 1969. – D. WILDENSTEIN, *Claude Monet, Biographie et Catalogue raisonné I*, Lausanne-Paris, 1974.

Exhibitions

1885: *Société des Pastellistes Français* (first year), Galerie Georges Petit, Paris. – **1886**: *Exposition Internationale du Blanc et Noir, Pastels et aquarelles*, Pavillon de l'Enseignement, Paris. – **1889**: *Société des Pastellistes Français*, Galerie Georges Petit, Paris. – **1896**: *Société des Pastellistes Français*, Galerie Georges Petit, Paris. – **1897**: *Société des Pastellistes Français*, Galerie Georges Petit, Paris. – **1898**: *Odilon Redon. Dessins et Pastels*, Galerie Ambroise Vollard, Paris. – **1901**: *Pastels et peintures d'Odilon Redon*, Galerie Ambroise Vollard, Paris. – **1902**: *The Annual Exhibition of Water-colors, Pastels and Miniatures by American Artists*, The Art Institute of Chicago; *Société des Pastellistes Français*, Galerie Georges Petit, Paris. – **1903**: *Pastels et Peintures d'Odilon Redon*, Galerie Durand-Ruel, Paris; *Société des Pastellistes Français*, Galerie Georges Petit, Paris. – **1904**:, *Société des Pastellistes Français*, Galerie Georges Petit, Paris. – **1908**: *Peintures, Pastels, Dessins et Lithographies par Odilon Redon*, Galerie Druet, Paris. – **1914**: *Degas, Peintures, pastels, dessins, estampes*, Galerie Ambroise Vollard, Paris. – **1918**: *Vente d'huiles, aquarelles, pastels et dessins provenant de l'atelier de Degas*, Galerie Georges Petit, Paris (May and December). – **1919**: *Vente d'estampes et monotypes provenant de l'atelier de Degas*, Galerie Manzi-Joyant, Paris (November). – **1921**: *Tableaux, pastels et gouaches*, Galerie Durand-Ruel, Paris. – **1928**: *Dessins et pastels par Camille Pissarro*, Galerie Marcel Bernheim, Paris. – **1930**: *Camille Pissarro, Centenaire de la naissance de l'artiste*, Orangerie des Tuileries, Paris. – **1931**: *Gouaches, Pastels and Drawings by Camille Pissarro*, Leicester Galleries, London. – **1949**: *Gauguin, Exposition du Centenaire*, Orangerie des Tuileries, Paris. – **1950**: *Gauguin et le groupe de Pont-Aven*, Musée des Beaux-Arts, Quimper. – **1951**: *Redon, Pastels and Drawings*, Seligmann Gallery, New York, Cleveland Museum of Art, Walker Art Center, Minneapolis. – **1953**: *Donation David Weill*, Orangerie des Tuileries, Paris. – **1955**: *Camille Pissarro: A Collection of Pastels and Studies*, Leicester Galleries, London. – **1956-1957**: *Odilon Redon*, Orangerie des Tuileries, Paris. – **1960**: *Paul Gauguin*, Haus der Kunst, Munich; *Dessins de J.-F. Millet*, Cabinet des Dessins, Louvre, Paris; *Berthe Morisot*, Wildenstein Gallery, New York; *Edouard Vuillard, peintures, aquarelles, dessins*, Musée Toulouse-Lautrec, Albi; *D'Ingres à nos jours. Aquarelles, pastels et dessins*, Galerie J. J. Bellier, Paris. – **1961**: *Edouard Vuillard*, Galerie Durand-Ruel, Paris. – **1964**: *Aquarelles, gouaches et pastels du XIXᵉ siècle à nos jours*, Musées Royaux des Beaux-Arts, Brussels; *Centenaire de Toulouse-Lautrec*, Palais de la Barbie, Albi; *Vuillard*, Kunsthaus, Zürich. – **1965**: *Boudin, Aquarelles et pastels*, Cabinet des Dessins, Louvre, Paris. – **1966**: *Gauguin and the Pont-Aven Group*, Tate Gallery, London. – **1967**: *Chefs-d'œuvre des Collections suisses de Manet à Picasso*, Orangerie des Tuileries, Paris. – **1968**: *Edouard Vuillard, K. X. Roussel*, Haus der Kunst, Munich and Orangerie des Tuileries, Paris; *Whistler, Paintings, Pastels...*, The Art Institute of Chicago. – **1969**: *Degas: Œuvres du Musée du Louvre. Peintures, Pastels, Dessins, Sculptures*, Orangerie des Tuileries, Paris; *Edvard Munch*, Musée des Arts Décoratifs, Paris. – **1973**: *Autour de Lévy-Dhurmer. Visionnaires et Intimistes en 1900*, Grand Palais, Paris; *Idéalistes et symbolistes*, Galerie J. C. Gaubert, Paris; *Gauguin Monotypes*, Philadelphia Museum of Art. – **1975**: *Degas*, Galerie Schmit, Paris. – **1975-1976**: *Millet*, Grand Palais, Paris and Hayward Gallery, London. – **1976**: *Degas*, Seibu Museum of Art, Tokyo; *Le Symbolisme en Europe*, Grand Palais, Paris. – **1977**: *De Burne-Jones à Bonnard. Dessins provenant du Musée National d'Art Moderne*, Cabinet des Dessins, Louvre, Paris. – **1978**: *Edgar Degas*, Aquavella Galleries, New York; *Selection of Drawings, Watercolours and Pastels by Camille Pissarro*, J. P. L. Fine Arts, London. – **1978-1979**: *French Drawings, Watercolors and Pastels, Collection L. Spangenberg*, Cincinnati Art Museum. – **1979**: *Degas*, National Gallery of Scotland, Edinburgh. – **1979-1980**: *The Crisis of Impressionism*, Museum of Art, Michigan University, Ann Arbor. – **1980**: *Fernand Khnopff*, Musée des Arts Décoratifs, Paris, Musées Royaux des Beaux-Arts, Brussels, Kunsthalle, Hamburg; *Le Pastel*, Château d'Ancy-le-Franc; *Post-Impressionism. Cross-Currents in European and American Painting (1880-1906)*, National Gallery, Washington. – **1980-1981**: *Pissarro*, Hayward Gallery, London, Grand Palais, Paris, Boston Museum of Fine Arts; *The Symbolist Aesthetic*, Museum of Modern Art. New York. – **1981**: *Mary Cassatt*, Isetan Museum of Art, Tokyo and Prefectural Museum of Art, Nara; *Eugène Boudin*, Galerie Schmit, Paris. – **1982**: *Pour mon plaisir, XIXᵉ et XXᵉ siècles*, Galerie Schmit, Paris. – **1983**: *Lumières sur la peinture, XIXᵉ-XXᵉ siècles, peintures et pastels, aquarelles, dessins et sculptures*, Galerie Schmit, Paris; *Pastels des XIXᵉ et XXᵉ siècles des Collections du Petit Palais*, Musée du Petit Palais, Paris. – **1983-1984**: *Manet*, Grand Palais, Paris, and Metropolitan Museum of Art, New York.

20th CENTURY

General Works and Monographs

ARAKAWA and M. GINS, *The Mechanism of Meaning*, New York, 1979.

A. CHASTEL, *Vuillard (1868-1940)*, Paris, 1946. – J. CLAIR, "Eloge du pastel" in *Considérations sur l'état des Beaux-Arts, critique de la Modernité*, Paris, 1983.

P. DAIX and G. BOUDAILLE, *Picasso, L'époque bleue et l'époque rose, Catalogue raisonné*, Neuchâtel, 1966. – P. DAIX and J. ROSSELET, *Le cubisme de Picasso, Catalogue raisonné de l'œuvre peint (1907-1916)*, Neuchâtel, 1979. – J. DUPIN, *Miró*, Paris, 1961.

FOUAD EL-ETR, "Esquisse d'un traité du pastel" in catalogue of the Sam Szafran exhibition, Geneva, 1974.

K. GABLER, *E. L. Kirchner, Dokumente: Fotos, Schriften, Briefe, Zeichnungen, Pastelle, Aquarelle*, 2 vols., Aschaffenburg, 1980. – C. GREENBERG, *Joan Miró*, New York, 1948. – W. GROHMANN, *Paul Klee*, New York, 1954.

B. HASKELL, *Arthur Dove*, San Francisco, 1974. – T. B. Hess, *Willem de Kooning*, New York, 1968.

M. KETTERER, W. HENZE, C. von MANTEUFFEL, H. BOLLIGER, *Ernst Ludwig Kirchner. Zeichnungen und Pastelle*, Stuttgart-Zurich, 1980 – A. KING, "Contemporary Drawings, Problems of Materials" in *New Drawing in America*, New York, 1982.

N. NANNI, "Frank Kupka et le symbolisme viennois" in *Cahiers du Musée National d'Art Moderne*, No. 5, Paris.

S. PRESTON, *Edouard Vuillard*, New York, n.d.

M. RAGON and A. VERDET, *Jean Atlan*, Geneva, 1960. – C. ROGER-MARX, *Vuillard et son temps*, Paris, 1946. – B. ROSE, *Drawing Now*, New York, 1976. – W. RUBIN, *Miró in the Collection of the Museum of Modern Art*, New York, 1973.

J. SALMON, *Vuillard*, Paris, 1945; *Vuillard, 12 pastels...*, Paris, 1966. – J. SALMON and A. VAILLANT, *Vuillard, Cahiers de dessins*, Paris, 1949.

Exhibitions

1958: *Fautrier*, Galerie 22, Düsseldorf; *Jean Fautrier*, Galleria Apollinaire, Milan. – **1959**: *Fautrier*, Galerie 22, Düsseldorf; *Jean Fautrier, Paintings, Gouaches, Drawings*, Hanover Gallery, London. – **1964**: *Vuillard*, Kunsthaus, Zürich. – **1966**: *Le Fauvisme français et les débuts de l'expressionnisme allemand*, Musée National d'Art Moderne, Paris and Haus der Kunst, Munich. – **1967**: *Wifredo Lam*, Stockholm Museet. – **1968**: *Vuillard und Roussel*, Haus der Kunst, Munich and Orangerie des Tuileries, Paris. – **1969**: *Jackson Pollock, Works on Paper*, Museum of Modern Art, New York; *Henri Michaux*, Von der Heydt-Museum, Wuppertal and Musée d'Art et d'Histoire, Saint-Etienne. – **1971**: *Arakawa*, Galleria Arturo Schwarz, Milan. – **1972**: *Douze ans d'art contemporain en France*, Grand Palais, Paris; *Szafran, Pastels (1970-1972)*, Galerie Claude Bernard, Paris; *Pierre Skira, Pastels*, Galerie du Dragon, Paris. – **1972-1973**: *Henri Michaux*, Kestner-Gesellschaft, Hanover. – **1973**: *Le Futurisme (1909-1916)*, Musée National d'Art Moderne, Paris. – **1974**: *Wifredo Lam. Œuvres de 1938 à 1946, en hommage à Pierre Loeb*, Galerie Albert Loeb, Paris; *Matta*, Kestner-Gesellschaft, Hanover; *Joan Miró*, Grand Palais, Paris; *Riopelle, Paintings from 1970-1973 and Le Roi de Thulé Series*, Pierre Matisse Gallery, New York; *Szafran (with Fouad El-Etr's Esquisse d'un traité du pastel)*, Galerie Artel, Geneva. – **1975**: *Matta. L'œil-être*, Galerie Iolas. Paris; *Jean-Paul Riopelle, Paintings from 1974 and Pastels from 1975*, Pierre Matisse Gallery, New York. – **1976**: *André Masson, 200 dessins*, Musée d'Art Moderne de la Ville de Paris; *Matta. Hommage aux Pyrénées*, Château de Castelnau; *Henri Michaux, peintures*, Fondation Maeght, Saint-Paul-de-Vence. – **1977**: *Arakawa*, Städtische Kunsthalle, Düsseldorf; *Le dessin*, Arc 2, Musée d'Art Moderne de la Ville de Paris; *Papiers sur nature*, Festival d'Automne, Paris; *Jean-Paul Riopelle, Grands Formats (1952-1975)*, Pierre Matisse Gallery, New York. – **1978**: *American Art at Mid-Century. The Subjects of the Artist*, National Gallery, Washington; *Matta, 55 dessins depuis 1937*, Galerie du Dragon, Paris; *Henri Michaux*, Musée National d'Art Moderne, Paris. – **1979**: *Arakawa*, Seibu Museum of Art, Tokyo; *Arakawa, Print Works (1965-1979)*, Museum of Art, Kitakyushu City; *Jackson Pollock, Drawing into Painting*, Musée d'Art Moderne de la Ville de Paris. – **1979-1980**: *Picasso, Œuvres reçues en paiement des droits de succession*, Grand Palais, Paris. – **1980**: *Atlan. Œuvres des collections publiques françaises*, Centre Georges Pompidou, Paris; *Dessins de la Fondation Maeght*, Fondation Maeght, Saint-Paul-de-Vence; *Paul Klee, Sammlung Felix Klee*, Kestner-Gesellschaft, Hanover; *Pablo Picasso, A Retrospective*, Museum of Modern Art, New York; *Sam Szafran, Pastels*, Galerie Claude Bernard, Paris; *Arakawa*, Galerie Maeght, Zürich. – **1981**: *Jean-Paul Riopelle, Peintures (1946-1977)*, Centre Georges Pompidou, Paris. – **1981-1982**: *Arakawa, Bilder und Zeichnungen (1962-1981)*, Kestner-Gesellschaft, Hanover. – **1982**: *Arakawa*, Galerie Maeght, Paris; *Guggenheim Venezia/New York. Sessanta Opere 1900-1950*, Pinacoteca Capitolina, Rome; *Pierre Skira, Pastels*, Galerie Etienne de Causans, Paris; *Peter Stämpfli*, Aargauer-Kunsthaus, Aarau; *Stämpfli*, Galerie Maeght, Zürich; *Titus-Carmel. Eclats et Caparaçons (1980-1982)*, Galerie Maeght, Paris. – **1983**: *Hommage à Wifredo Lam*, Museo Nacional de Arte Contemporáneo, Madrid, Musée d'Art Moderne de la Ville de Paris, Musée d'Ixelles, Brussels; *André Masson*, Galerie Patrice Trigano, Paris; *André Masson, 67 œuvres 1948-1953*, Galerie Louise Leiris, Paris.

List of illustrations

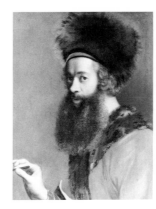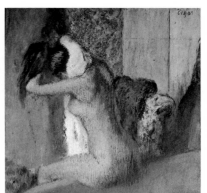

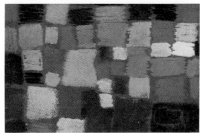

Details of these three pictures
are reproduced on
the following pages:

Index of names and places

SKIRA

TEXT AND PLATES PRINTED BY
IRL IMPRIMERIES RÉUNIES LAUSANNE S.A.

BINDING BY
MAYER & SOUTTER S.A., RENENS-LAUSANNE

Printed in Switzerland